EVERY DOLLAR MAKES A DIFFERENCE

the
better
world
SHOPPING
GUIDE

Ellis Jones

NEW SOCIETY PUBLISHERS

Cataloging in Publication Data:
A catalog record for this publication is available from the National Library of Canada.

Copyright © 2010 by Ellis Jones. All rights reserved.

Cover concept by Ellis Jones. Design by Diane McIntosh.
Images: Getty Images/Photodisc Green.

Printed in Canada.

Paperback ISBN: 978-0-86571-680-3
eISBN: 978-1-55092-463-3

Inquiries regarding requests to reprint all or part of
The Better World Shopping Guide should be addressed to
New Society Publishers at the address below.

To order directly from the publishers, please call toll-free
(North America) 1-800-567-6772, or order online at
www.newsociety.com

Any other inquiries can be directed by mail to:
New Society Publishers
P.O. Box 189, Gabriola Island, BC V0R 1X0, Canada
1-800-567-6772

New Society Publishers' mission is to publish books that contribute in fundamental ways to building an ecologically sustainable and just society, and to do so with the least possible impact on the environment, in a manner that models this vision. We are committed to doing this not just through education, but through action. Our printed, bound books are printed on Forest Stewardship Council-certified acid-free paper that is **100% post-consumer recycled** (100% old growth forest-free), processed chlorine free, and printed with vegetable-based, low-VOC inks, with covers produced using FSC-certified stock. New Society also works to reduce its carbon footprint, and purchases carbon offsets based on an annual audit to ensure a carbon neutral footprint. For further information, or to browse our full list of books and purchase securely, visit our website at: www.newsociety.com

NEW SOCIETY PUBLISHERS

www.newsociety.com

Mixed Sources
Cert no. SW-COC-001271
© 1996 FSC

FSC

Contents

APPRECIATION

I am very grateful to Paul Todisco, Collin Ahrens, Jason Logan, Brett Jacobs, Jacob O'Brien and Warren Zeger for their hard work testing the guide and researching brands in the real world, and to my wife, Ara Francis, for her unwavering advocacy and dedication to getting this project the recognition and support it deserves. Also, a very special thank you to the good people at Christie Communications who have been incredible in making important connections for me around this work.

I am also very grateful to you, the reader, for picking up this book. I'd like to say (because you may never hear it from anyone else) on behalf of all of the people on this planet whom you will never meet and all the natural places you will never see...

Thank you.

3RD EDITION NOTES

As I write this sentence, I must admit that I am still completely amazed at the idea that this little book has sold nearly 90,000 copies! I am deeply inspired when I think of the tens of thousands of people who have decided that the time has come to bring democracy to our economy.

After surviving company collapses, oil spills, and taxpayer bailouts, we're finally beginning to understand the deep connection between our economic and our political lives. In order to bring real change to this situation you'll need the best tools available to you. In this edition you'll find :

✓ More than 1500 companies evaluated
✓ Now over 50 sources of reliable data
✓ New research (Hotels, Online, Insurance)
✓ More Top 10 Lists (Bailouts, Lobbying)
✓ An expanded 20 Best List & 20 Worst List
✓ An iPhone App! (not included)

Let's reclaim our democracy.

THE WEBSITE

This guide is far too small to contain the wide range of data that goes into generating the rankings for each company. If you are interested in more specifics on how individual companies are rated, and exactly what is taken into account, you can visit the website. It also contains updated rankings, direct links to resources, and new product categories that have been added since the writing of this guide.

One other note that may be of interest to some of you is the release of an iPhone App called "Better World Shopper" based on the same data. While it does not provide all of the useful information you'll find in this book, it does give you instant access to all of the rankings. Having this information at your fingertips can turn out to be really useful, particularly when you forget to bring the book with you!

Learn more about the research behind this work and take a peek at the iphone app online at:

www.betterworldshopper.org

THE PROBLEM

Money is power. Perhaps more than any generation that has come before us, we understand the deeply-rooted reality of this short phrase and its universal meaning for every human being living on this planet.

It follows that wherever large amounts of money collect, so also new centers of power form. The latest historical manifestation of this is the modern corporation. As trillions of dollars accumulate in the corporate sphere, we witness the growing power of corporations to shape the world as they see fit.

This power is not limited to controlling the face of our own government through consistent, record-breaking, campaign contributions, but also the fate of millions of people and the planet itself through jobs, resource exploitation, pollution, working conditions, energy consumption, forest destruction, and so on.

Make no mistake, these new power centers are not democracies. We don't vote for the CEO's or their policies (unless we are rich enough to be significant shareholders, who are informed enough to know what's going on, and compassionate enough to care about more than just personal profit), yet our destinies are increasingly in their hands.

THE SOLUTION

As these power centers shift, we must shift our own voices if we wish to be heard. As citizens, on average, we might vote once every four years, if at all. As consumers, we vote every single day with the purest form of power...money. The average American family spends around $18,000 every year on goods and services. Think of it as casting 18,000 votes every year for the kind of world you want to live in.

Unfortunately, as difficult as it is to find good, solid information on candidates during an election year, it's often even harder to find good, solid information on corporations. Our current laws are so lax, that half of the time we can't even figure out which brands belong to which companies (they don't have to tell us), much less have any idea of what their business practices look like.

For the past decade, I've dedicated myself to researching this very problem by compiling a database of every reliable source of information available on corporate behavior, and synthesizing the information into a single report card grade for every company. The result is this book. Use it to reclaim your true vote. Use it to build a better world.

THE ISSUES

➤ **HUMAN RIGHTS:** sweatshops, third-world community exploitation, international health issues, economic divestment, child labor, worker health & safety records, union busting, fair wages, fatalities, democratic principles.

➤ **THE ENVIRONMENT:** global warming, toxic waste dumping, rainforest destruction, pollution, recycling, renewable energy, eco-innovations, sustainable farming, greenwashing, resource conservation.

➤ **ANIMAL PROTECTION:** humane treatment, animal testing, utilization of alternatives, factory farming, animal habitat preservation, sustainable harvesting, ecosystem impacts.

➤ **COMMUNITY INVOLVEMENT:** volunteer efforts, local business support, sustainable growth, family farms, donations, nonprofit alliances, campaign contributions, paid lobbyists, political corruption.

➤ **SOCIAL JUSTICE:** class action lawsuits, unethical business practices, government fines, cover-ups, illegal activities, transparency, harassment, discrimination based on race, gender, age, sexuality, ability, religion, ethnicity.

THE SOURCES

Here is a short list of some of the resources used to assess the overall social responsibility of the companies included in this guide:

[BBB]   Better Business Bureau: Torch Awards

[BE]   Business Ethics: 100 Best Corporate Citizens

[CPI]   Center for Public Integrity: Lobby Watch

[GAM]   Green America: Green Business Certification

[CCC]   Clean Computer Campaign

[CC]   Climate Counts

[CEP]   Council on Economic Priorities

[CER]   Covalence Ethical Rankings

[CK]   Corporate Knights: 100 Most Sustainable Corporations

[CW]   Corpwatch: Greenwash Awards

[EC]   Ethical Consumer: Rankings & Boycotts

[EPA]   The US Environmental Protection Agency

[FT]   Transfair USA: Fair Trade Certification

[GP]   Greenpeace: Guide to Green Electronics

[HRC]   Human Rights Campaign: Equality Index

[MM]   Multinational Monitor: 100 Worst Corporations

[RS]   Responsible Shopper: Responsibility Rankings

For a more comprehensive list visit: www.betterworldshopper.org

THE RANKINGS

STEP 1: Over 20 years worth of data is collected from a wide range of public, private, and nonprofit sources tracking information on one or more of the five issue areas that make up the overall responsibility picture for companies that create the products and services we use every day.

STEP 2: The data is organized into a massive database of more than 1000 companies that matches each individual company with its brands, assigns appropriate weights to each piece of data based on its quality, reliability, and scope, and calculates an overall social and environmental responsibility score for each company from –50 to +50.

STEP 3: Companies and brands are transferred to smaller, more specific data charts based on common product categories where each is assigned a letter grade based on its overall responsibility relative to its competitors in the same product category. This relative grading system allows consumers to maximize the impact of their dollars regardless of what they're purchasing.

THE RANKINGS

STEP 4: Researchers are sent to supermarkets, natural foods stores, and retail outlets across the country to identify those products which are most commonly available to the average consumer to make sure that what you see on the shelves matches what you see in the book. Those particular companies/brands are then transferred into the easy-to-use report cards that make up the bulk of the shopping guide.

STEP 5: As regular data sources release their latest findings, they are added to the database. Also, as new third-party sources of data are identified, they are evaluated for potential inclusion in the ranking system. Mergers and buyouts are tracked so that their effects on the rankings can be noted. Updated rankings are regularly made available online through the website until a new edition of the shopping guide can be published.

As readers, your comments and suggestions are invaluable. Please contact me if you have ideas on how to improve the ranking system.

contact@betterworldshopper.org

BEST COMPANY PROFILE (BANKS)

SHOREBANK

☆ Green America Certified Green Business
☆ Social Venture Network member
☆ A Certified "B Corporation"
☆ Community Investing Award Winner
☆ Social Capitalist Award Winner

☆ Worked closely with Muhammad Yunus,
   Nobel Peace Prize Winner, microfinance
☆ Financed renovation of more than
   51,000 affordable housing units
☆ Developed Sustainability Scoring
   System for loan projects
☆ Environmentally Responsible,
   Community Development Bank
☆ Offers Socially Responsible Credit Cards

OVERALL GRADE: A+

www.sbk.com
www.eco-bank.com

WORST COMPANY PROFILE (BANKS)

CITIBANK

- ☠ Recipient, Corporate Shame Award[3]
- ☠ Worst overall ranking in industry[43]
- ☠ Worst Corporations List for 2 years[38]
- ☠ 'D' for social & environmental impacts[52]
- ☠ Overall ethics rating of VERY POOR[22]
- ☠ $50 billion paid by us to bailout[41]
- ☠ $74 million paid to political lobbyists[8]
- ☠ $27 million in campaign contributions[9]

- ☠ $2.7 billion to settle WorldCom fraud[41]
- ☠ SEC — Citi helped Enron commit fraud[36]
- ☠ Sued for selling worthless Enron stock[43]
- ☠ Paid largest settlement in FTC history[36]
- ☠ GAO — negligent of money laundering[49]
- ☠ $70 million paid for unfair lending [43]

OVERALL GRADE: F

*For more details you can look up the source reference
number in the DATA SOURCES section in the back.*

THE 20 BEST LIST

1. SEVENTH GENERATION
2. METHOD
3. ORGANIC VALLEY
4. CLIF BAR
5. AVEDA
6. TOM'S OF MAINE
7. DR. BRONNER'S
8. KING ARTHUR FLOUR
9. EARTHBOUND FARM
10. DANSKO FOOTWEAR
11. PATAGONIA
12. WORKING ASSETS
13. NEW BELGIUM BREWING
14. NANCY'S DAIRY & SOY
15. ENDANGERED SPECIES CHOC.
16. HONEST TEA
17. EARTH FRIENDLY
18. ANNIE'S NATURALS
19. EDEN FOODS
20. BEN & JERRY'S

Rankings are based on overall social and environmental records

THE 20 WORST LIST

1. EXXON-MOBIL
2. KRAFT (& ALTRIA)
3. WAL-MART
4. CHEVRON-TEXACO
5. GENERAL ELECTRIC
6. GENERAL MOTORS
7. NESTLE
8. PFIZER
9. CITIBANK
10. AIG
11. MICROSOFT
12. ARCHER DANIELS MIDLAND
13. VERIZON
14. PROCTOR & GAMBLE
15. FORD
16. DILLARD'S
17. V.F. (VANITY FAIR)
18. UNITED AIRLINES
19. SEARS
20. BANK OF AMERICA

Rankings are based on overall social and environmental records

THE 10 SMALL BUT BEAUTIFUL LIST

1. SHOREBANK PACIFIC
2. NEW LEAF PAPER
3. GUAYAKI
4. BETTER WORLD TELECOM
5. NUMI TEA
6. ALTER ECO
7. RECYCLINE (PRESERVE)
8. EQUAL EXCHANGE
9. TEN THOUSAND VILLAGES
10. BETTER WORLD CLUB

The above list includes 10 small companies you may not have heard of that are true social and environmental leaders in their industries.

THE TOP 10 THINGS TO CHANGE

1. BANK
2. GASOLINE
3. SUPERMARKET
4. RETAIL STORES
5. CAR
6. SEAFOOD
7. CHOCOLATE
8. COFFEE / TEA
9. CREDIT CARDS
10. CLEANING PRODUCTS

If you want to begin with the changes that will make the most difference for people and the planet, start with these ten things.

THE TOP 10 BAILOUT LIST

1.	AIG	70
2.	CITIBANK	50
3.	BANK OF AMERICA	45
4.	GENERAL MOTORS	31
5.	JP MORGAN	25
6.	WELLS FARGO	25
7.	CHRYSLER	12
8.	MORGAN STANLEY	10
9.	GOLDMAN SACHS	10
10.	PNC FINANCIAL	8

We are quickly learning that unless we can keep companies responsible in the marketplace, we may end up paying for their irresponsible behavior with taxpayer dollars.

The above list includes the 10 companies that, as of May 2009, received the most bailout money from the US taxpayers. The figures on the right represent how much we have spent, *in billions*, bailing these companies out.[41]

THE TOP 10 LOBBYIST LIST

1. GENERAL ELECTRIC	196
2. KRAFT (& ALTRIA)	178
3. AT&T	151
4. EXXON MOBIL	139
5. BLUE CROSS/SHIELD	136
6. VERIZON	133
7. GENERAL MOTORS	93
8. PFIZER	93
9. FORD	90
10. MICROSOFT	89

Its important to understand that we are not the only ones learning to turn our dollars into votes. These are some of the loudest economic voices in Washington.

The above list includes 10 companies currently spending some of the largest amounts of money on Washington lobbyists to influence the democratic process in ways that serve their own interests. The figures on the right represent how much they have spent, *in millions*, over the last decade.[9]

WHAT DO THE GRADES MEAN?

A	Often these companies were created specifically to provide socially and environmentally responsible options for consumers. A handful are merely responsibility leaders in their industry.
B	These companies tend to represent mainstream companies that are making significant progress in turning toward more people/planet friendly behaviors.
C	Companies that fall in the middle either have mixed responsibility records or insufficient data exists to rank them relative to the other companies.
D	If a company ends up here, it is involved in practices that have significantly negative consequences for humans and the environment.
F	This category is reserved for companies that are actively participating in the rapid destruction of the planet and the exploitation of human beings. Avoid these products at all costs.

WHAT IS ALL THIS EXTRA STUFF?

WHAT YOU NEED TO KNOW
This section will give you a thumbnail sketch of the current industry and its impact.

BUYING TIPS
Here you'll see tips that should help you maximize the positive impact of your dollar.

GREEN HERO
Company X

Examples of just a few of the things that put this particular company head and shoulders above the rest.

CORPORATE VILLAIN
Company Y

Examples of some of the things that land this company squarely at the bottom of the rankings.

RESOURCES
Here you'll find web links to sites that provide you with more information on the best companies or practices.

WHAT IF I CAN'T FIND A COMPANY?

While this guide is meant to be comprehensive, it is far from complete. You will likely encounter companies and brands on the shelves that don't show up in these pages. Here are a few simple guidelines that should help you:

If an unknown company's products are certified fair trade, you may assume that it falls into the A range.

If an unknown company's products are certified organic, you may assume that it falls into the B+ range.

If you don't know anything at all about a particular company or brand, assume that it falls into the C range.

Unknown companies producing clothing and shoes should be assumed to have a D or F.

If you wish to see a more detailed version of these rankings or ask about a particular company that you can't find in the guide, you're welcome to visit:

www.betterworldshopper.org

HOW TO USE THIS SHOPPING GUIDE

This book is meant to be used as a practical guide while shopping at the supermarket, in the mall, or online. Familiarize yourself with the alphabetical listing of categories and "dog-ear" any pages you find particularly useful.

Utilize the rankings on the left as a quick guide to any product you're thinking about buying. Note that all rankings are relative to their product category so that a company may shift up or down depending on its competition.

Useful information and helpful tips appear on the right along with a quick sketch of some of the differences between the best and worst companies. At the bottom of the page are links to online resources to learn more about some of the companies listed.

The book has been purposefully made small so that you can keep it with you in your purse, backpack, briefcase, or pocket. Find a convenient place for it now, while you're reading this sentence. Whatever you do, don't put it on a shelf!

AIRLINES

A	**A+**	
	A	
	A–	
B	**B+**	JetBlue
	B	Southwest, Midwest, Virgin
	B–	Alaska Air, Horizon
C	**C+**	Frontier
	C	Japan Airlines, Lufthansa, Qantas, Spirit, Air France, British Airways, Cathay Pacific, Singapore
	C–	KLM, Korean
D	**D+**	Continental, Express Jet, SkyWest
	D	AirTran, Delta
	D–	American Airlines, American Eagle
F	**F**	United, US Airways

AIRLINES

WHAT YOU NEED TO KNOW
Air travel has become so ubiquitous in our modern society that we often forget its significant environmental impact.

BUYING TIPS
✓ Green travel org's now offer carbon offsets to eliminate your flight's greenhouse gas impact

GREEN HERO

JetBlue

☆ Perfect 100 on HRC Equality Index
☆ Industry leader in treatment of passengers
☆ Offers carbon offsets & green food options

CORPORATE VILLAIN

United

☠ RS "F" for recycling efforts in the industry
☠ Paid $29 million to Washington lobbyists
☠ Named global climate change laggard

RESOURCES
🖥 www.sustainabletravelinternational.org
🖥 www.terrapass.com

APPLIANCES & HARDWARE

A	**A+**	Preserve, Recycline, TerraCycle
	A	Old Fashioned Milk Paint
	A−	
B	**B+**	
	B	3M, Ace Hardware
	B−	Owens Corning
C	**C+**	Whirlpool, Dyson, Stanley, DeWalt, JCB, Dremel, Tefal, Rubbermaid, Dupont, Norelco, Conair, Admiral, Kitchenaid, Cuisinart, Magic Chef, Hoover, Dirt Devil, Maytag, Bissell
	C	DeLonghi, Wahl, Haier, Electrolux, Krups, Sunbeam, Remington, Sanyo, Sylvania, Panasonic, Frigidaire
	C−	Siemens
D	**D+**	Black & Decker, Samsung, Emerson, Philips, Bosch, Hitachi
	D	Lowe's, Sherwin Williams
	D−	Home Depot, Costco, LG
F	**F**	Sears, Walmart, Braun, Craftsman, Daewoo, Kenmore, GE

APPLIANCES & HARDWARE

WHAT YOU NEED TO KNOW
Whether it's major home improvement efforts or just small kitchen appliances, the hardware you buy for your house has a significant impact on the people abroad that help manufacture it.

BUYING TIPS
✓ Look for products with Energy Star labels

CORPORATE VILLAIN
Walmart
☠ MM's "Worst Corporation" list for 3 years
☠ Major toxic waste dumping fines
☠ CEP "F" for overall social responsibility
☠ Documented exploitation of child labor

CORPORATE VILLAIN
GE (General Electric)
☠ MM's "Worst Corporation" list for 4 years
☠ #34 in "Top 100 Corporate Criminals"
☠ Target of "War Profiteer" campaign
☠ Paid $196 million to Washington lobbyists

RESOURCES
🖥 www.energystar.gov

BABY CARE

A	**A+**	Seventh Generation
	A	Aubrey Organics, gDiapers, Healthy Times, Peapods, Nubius Organics
	A–	Tushies, Earth's Best, Earth Mama, Organic Baby, Tender Care
B	**B+**	Nature's Gate, Avalon Organics, Weleda, Jason, Sesame Street
	B	Aveeno, Huggies, Pull-Ups, Johnson & Johnson, GoodNites
	B–	Horizon Organics
C	**C+**	Enfamil, Oshkosh
	C	Mr. Bubble, Burt's Bees, Baby Magic, Pure n' Gentle, Beech-Nut, Graco, Munchkin
	C–	Avent, Evenflo
D	**D+**	Coppertone, Playtex, Del Monte
	D	Pedialyte, Pediasure, Similac, Church & Dwight, Q-Tips, Vaseline
	D–	Chiquita
F	**F**	Nabisco, Gerber, Nestle, Disney, Luvs, Under Jams, Easy Ups, Pampers, Baby Einstein

BABY CARE

WHAT YOU NEED TO KNOW
Infants and toddlers are more vulnerable to the effects of harmful chemicals and pesticides, so if you're going to buy anything organic, it should be something from this category.

GREEN HERO

Seventh Generation

☆ Ranked #1 best company on the planet
☆ Empowers consumers w/packaging
☆ Winner, Sustainability Report Award
☆ Socially Responsible Business Award

CORPORATE VILLAIN

Gerber (Nestle)

☠ Baby formula human rights boycott
☠ "Most Irresponsible" corporation award
☠ Involved in child slavery lawsuit
☠ Aggressive takeovers of family farms

RESOURCES
🖥 www.seventhgen.com
🖥 www.healthytimes.com
🖥 www.earthmamaangelbaby.com
🖥 www.gdiapers.com
🖥 www.earthsbest.com
🖥 www.tushies.com

BAKED GOODS & BAKING SUPPLIES

A	**A+**	King Arthur, Eden
	A	Rapunzel, Nature's Path
	A−	Bob's Red Mill, Ener-G, Spectrum
B	**B+**	Vermont Bread Co, Arrowhead Mills, SunSpire, Betty Crocker, Pillsbury, Gold Medal, Bisquick, Progresso, Hain, Quaker
	B	
	B−	
C	**C+**	Keebler, Kellogg's
	C	Ghirardelli, Krusteaz, Duncan Hines, Karo, Mother's, Eagle Brand, Sun Maid, Baker's, Diamond Walnut, Dr. Oetker, Borden, Hershey's, Cake Mate, Hodgson Mills, Entenmann's
	C−	Little Debbie
D	**D+**	Contadina
	D	Arm & Hammer, Hostess
	D−	Banquet
F	**F**	Jell-O, Nabisco, Kraft, Planters, Nestle, Carnation, Albers, Libby's

BAKED GOODS & BAKING SUPPLIES

BUYING TIPS
✓ Buy organic baking products when available

GREEN HERO

King Arthur Flour

☆ 100% employee-owned company
☆ Business Ethics award winner
☆ BBB's Torch Award for ethics

CORPORATE VILLAIN

Jell-O (Kraft)

☠ MM's "Worst Corporation" list for 5 years
☠ Currently target of 2 major boycotts
☠ Greenwash Award for public deception
☠ Named global climate change laggard
☠ Paid $178* million to Washington lobbyists

RESOURCES
🖳 www.edenfoods.com
🖳 www.kingarthurflour.com
🖳 www.rapunzel.com
🖳 www.naturespath.com
🖳 www.bobsredmill.com

BANKS & CREDIT CARDS

A	**A+**	ShoreBank, ShoreBank Pacific, University Bank, VanCity Credit Union, New Resource Bank
	A	Chittenden, Wainwright, Albina Community, City First, Franklin
	A−	Working Assets, Green America, Brighter Planet
B	**B+**	
	B	LOCAL CREDIT UNIONS
	B−	
C	**C+**	American Express, ING, HSBC
	C	Mastercard, VISA
	C−	Sovereign, UBS, Credit Suisse
D	**D+**	KeyBank, Discover, Diners Club, Regions, US Bank, Capital One
	D	Wachovia, Citizens, Wells Fargo, JP Morgan, SunTrust, Comerica, Chase, Fifth Third, Barclay's
	D−	National City, PNC
F	**F**	Citibank, MBNA, Bank Of America

BANKS & CREDIT CARDS

WHAT YOU NEED TO KNOW

Where you put your money when you're not spending it is just as important as responsibly choosing what you spend it on. For your whole life (even while you sleep), that money will either be building a better world or tearing it down. While shopping, make each purchase doubly effective by using a credit card that donates a percentage of your purchases (over $5500/yr for the average American) to saving the planet.

BUYING TIPS

✓ Try using both a local bank AND an 'A' bank
✓ Find out which credit unions are in your area
✓ Switch to a socially responsible credit card

RESOURCES

🖥 www.sbk.com
🖥 www.universitybank.com
🖥 www.newresourcebank.com
🖥 www.creditunion.coop/cu_locator
🖥 www.eco-bank.com/cards
🖥 www.workingassets.com/creditcard
🖥 www.communityinvest.org

BEER

A	**A+**	New Belgium
	A	Wolaver's, Sierra Nevada
	A–	Eel River, Butte Creek, Peak, Bison, ORGANIC / LOCAL BREWERIES
B	**B+**	Samuel Smith's, St. Peter's
	B	Allagash, Rogue, Full Sail, Pyramid, Anchor Steam, Harpoon, Alaskan
	B–	Widmer, Redhook, Samuel Adams, Pabst Blue Ribbon
C	**C+**	Coors, Molson, Killian's, Blue Moon, Keystone, Amstel, Heineken, Asahi
	C	Guinness, Harp, Pacifico, Newcastle Brown, Corona, Modelo
	C–	Miller, Carlsburg, Mickey's, Hamm's, Milwaukee's Best, Foster's, Grolsch, Blue Moon, Leinenkugel
D	**D+**	
	D	Bass, Michelob, Busch, King Cobra, Becks, Budweiser, Stella Artois, Lowenbrau, Rolling Rock
	D–	
F	**F**	

BEER

BUYING TIPS
✓ Look for organic varieties of beer
✓ Buy from local microbreweries when possible
✓ Avoid buying beer in plastic bottles

GREEN HERO

New Belgium

☆ 1st 100% wind-powered brewery
☆ Conserves 50% more water vs. average
☆ An employee-owned business
☆ $1.6 million donated to local community

CORPORATE VILLAIN

Budweiser (Anheuser-Busch)

☠ #41 of PERI 100 Most Toxic Air Polluters
☠ Paid $12 million to Washington lobbyists
☠ EC overall responsibility rating of POOR

RESOURCES
🖥 www.newbelgium.com
🖥 www.sierranevada.com
🖥 www.ottercreekbrewing.com
🖥 www.beertown.com

BODY CARE

A	**A+**	Druide, Preserve, Dr. Bronner's, Tweezerman, Method
	A	Tom's of Maine, Aveda, Aubrey, Kiss My Face, EO, Auromere, EcoLips, Pangea, Body Shop
	A–	Lush, Dr Hauschka, NOW
B	**B+**	Pure & Basic, Ecco Bella, Giovanni, Jason, Alba, Nature's Gate, Shikai
	B	Avalon, Desert Essence, Crystal, Colgate, Speed Stick, Mennen
	B–	Lubriderm, Aveeno, Neutrogena, Purell, Clean & Clear
C	**C+**	St. Ive's, Keri, Curel
	C	Ban, Jergens, Blistex, Biore, Edge, Barbasol, Burt's Bees, Banana Boat
	C–	
D	**D+**	Mitchum, Coppertone, Nivea, Bic
	D	L'Oreal, Arrid, Arm & Hammer, Dove, Suave, Vaseline, Degree, Axe
	D–	
F	**F**	Chapstick, Schick, Noxema, Dial, Old Spice, Secret, Sure, Gillette, Olay, Right Guard, Dry Idea, Soft & Dri

BODY CARE

BUYING TIPS
✓ Avoid products tested on animals
✓ Seek out items made with organic
   ingredients
✓ Look for recyclable containers — #1, #2
   plastic
✓ Buy larger quantities to reduce packaging

GREEN HERO

Tom's Of Maine

☆ Powered by 100% renewable energy
☆ Gives 10% of profits to nonprofits
☆ Ranked #6 best company on the planet

CORPORATE VILLAIN

Chapstick (Wyeth)

☠ #93 in "Top 100 Corporate Criminals"
☠ MM's "Worst Corporation" list for 2 years
☠ Paid $29 million to Washington lobbyists

RESOURCES
🖥 www.tomsofmaine.com
🖥 www.druide.ca
🖥 www.recycline.com
🖥 www.drbronner.com
🖥 www.methodhome.com

BREAD

A	**A+**	LOCAL BAKERY
	A	Alvarado St Bakery, Nature's Path
	A–	Ener-G, Rudi's Organic, Food For Life, French Meadow Organic, Vermont Bread Co., Barowsky's
B	**B+**	Great Harvest Bread Co.
	B	Gold Medal, Pillsbury, Betty Crocker, FiberOne, Country Kitchen, Colombo
	B–	Pepperidge Farm
C	**C+**	Sun-Maid
	C	Country Hearth, Boboli, Oroweat, Milton's, Roman Meal, Tia Rosa, Thomas', Lender's, Van De Kamp's, Mission, Arnold
	C–	Sara Lee, Rainbo, Earth Grains, Weight Watchers, Ball Park
D	**D+**	
	D	Wonder, Home Pride, Nature's Pride
	D–	Alexia
F	**F**	Kraft, Stove-Top

BREAD

WHAT YOU NEED TO KNOW
Despite all of our technological advancement,
it's still a challenge to find a good, socially
responsible loaf of bread in the supermarket.

BUYING TIPS
✓ Support a local bakery in your community

GREEN HERO

Alvarado Street Bakery

☆ Worker-owned cooperative
☆ PC socially responsible business award
☆ GAM certified Green Business

CORPORATE VILLAIN

Wonder (Interstate Bakeries)

☠ Major racial discrimination law suit
☠ Refuses disclosure to consumers
☠ CEP "F" for overall social responsibility

RESOURCES
🖳 www.alvaradostreetbakery.com
🖳 www.rudisbakery.com
🖳 www.foodforlife.com

BREAKFAST FOOD

A	**A+**	
	A	Amy's Kitchen, Nature's Path, Envirokidz, Lifestream
	A–	Van's, Batter Blaster
B	**B+**	Shelton's
	B	General Mills, Betty Crocker, Pillsbury, Quaker, Ian's
	B–	
C	**C+**	Morningstar Farms, Eggo, Kashi, Kellogg's, Aunt Jemima, Armour, Smucker's
	C	Entenmann's, Krusteaz, Farm Rich, Hershey's, Weight Watchers, Hungry Jack
	C–	Jimmy Dean, Bob Evans
D	**D+**	Hormel, Ore-Ida
	D	Golden Griddle, Skippy
	D–	PAM, Banquet, Kudos
F	**F**	Nestle, Boca

BREAKFAST FOOD

WHAT YOU NEED TO KNOW
Every morning of your life, what you put on
your plate for breakfast will determine what
kind of world your children inherit in the future.

BUYING TIPS
✓ Buy at least one organic item for breakfast

GREEN HERO

Amy's Kitchen

☆ Donates food to relief efforts
☆ Produces all-vegetarian, organic foods
☆ GAM certified Green Business

CORPORATE VILLAIN

Banquet (ConAgra)

☠ #50 in "Top 100 Corporate Criminals"
☠ Ceres "Climate Change Laggard"
☠ CEP "F" for overall social responsibility

RESOURCES
🖥 www.amyskitchen.com
🖥 www.envirokidz.com
🖥 www.naturespath.com

BUTTER & MARGARINE

A	**A+**	Organic Valley
	A	Organic Pastures, Straus Family
	A–	Spectrum
B	**B+**	Clover Stornetta, Smart Balance, Earth Balance
	B	Tillamook, Cabot
	B–	
C	**C+**	Challenge
	C	Horizon Organic, Canoleo, Nucoa, Crystal, Kerrygold, Cloverleaf, Saffola, Canola Harvest, Benecol
	C–	Land O' Lakes
D	**D+**	
	D	Brummel & Brown, I Can't Believe It's Not Butter, Willow Run, Shedd's, Country Crock, Imperial, Promise
	D–	Blue Bonnet, Fleischmann's, Parkay
F	**F**	

BUTTER & MARGARINE

BUYING TIPS
✓ Look for "No Hormones" and "No Antibiotics"
✓ Seek out items made with organic ingredients
✓ Avoid hydrogenated, saturated, and trans fats

GREEN HERO

Organic Valley

☆ Small family farmer-owned co-operative
☆ Gives 10% of profits to local community
☆ Humane animal treatment a priority
☆ Ranked #3 best company on the planet

CORPORATE VILLAIN

Parkay (ConAgra)

☠ #50 in "Top 100 Corporate Criminals"
☠ CEP "F" for overall social responsibility
☠ Ceres "Climate Change Laggard"

RESOURCES
🖥 www.organicvalley.coop
🖥 www.strausmilk.com
🖥 www.organicpastures.com
🖥 www.cornucopia.org

CANDY, GUM & MINTS

A	**A+**	
	A	Glee Gum, Pure Fun, Sencha Natural
	A –	Speakeasy, Hain, Ginger People, St. Claire's, College Farm Organic
B	**B+**	Newman's Own Organic, Xylichew
	B	Reed's
	B –	Panda, Haribo, La Vie
C	**C+**	Jolly Ranchers, Good & Plenty, Hershey's, Andes, Heath, Twizzlers, Kit Kat, Almond Joy, Tootsie Roll, Mounds, Reese's, York, Charm's
	C	Red Vines, Mike & Ike, Werthers, Tic Tacs, Mentos, Riesen, Almond Roca
	C –	Jelly Belly
D	**D+**	
	D	Cadbury, Certs, Dentyne, Trident
	D –	Twix, Starburst, Skittles, M&Ms, Snickers, Milky Way, 3 Musketeers, LifeSavers, Mars, Extra, Orbit
F	**F**	Kraft, Trolli, Nerds, Laffy Taffy, Nestle, Daim, Butterfinger, Wonka, SweeTarts, After Eight, Nips

CANDY, GUM & MINTS

BUYING TIPS

Most major candy manufacturers are also major chocolate purchasers, which currently means that they are using child slave labor to produce much of their candy. It's important to keep these companies accountable until they agree to basic human rights standards in the industry.

GREEN HERO

Glee Gum

☆ GAM certified Green Business
☆ Uses wild-harvested rainforest plants
☆ Actively supports environmental groups

CORPORATE VILLAIN

M&Ms (Mars)

☠ On MM's "10 Worst Corporations" list
☠ Evidence that suppliers use child slave labor
☠ Target of fair trade campaign

RESOURCES

🖥 www.gleegum.com
🖥 www.econaturalsolutions.com
🖥 www.gingerpeople.com

CANNED BEANS, CHILI & STEWS

A	**A+**	Eden Foods
	A	Amy's
	A–	Walnut Acres, Westbrae, Bearitos
B	**B+**	Shelton's
	B	Old El Paso, Hamburger Helper, Progresso
	B–	Campbell's
C	**C+**	
	C	Bush's, B&M, Nalley, Ortega, GOYA
	C–	
D	**D+**	Hormel, S&W, Stagg, Dinty Moore, Heinz
	D	Knorr
	D–	Dennison's, Rosarita, Van Camp's, Marie Callender's
F	**F**	Libby's, Taco Bell

CANNED BEANS, CHILI & STEWS

WHAT YOU NEED TO KNOW
Some of the most socially responsible companies now provide a wide variety of canned goods that should be available at most supermarkets.

GREEN HERO

Eden Foods

☆ Ranked #19 best company on the planet
☆ CEP's highest social responsibility score
☆ GAM certified Green Business

CORPORATE VILLAIN

Hormel

☠ Supports inhumane factory farming
☠ Low score on HRC Equality Index
☠ Refuses disclosure to consumers

RESOURCES
🖥 www.edenfoods.com
🖥 www.amyskitchen.com
🖥 www.westbrae.com
🖥 www.walnutacres.com

CANNED FRUIT & VEGETABLES

A	**A+**	Eden Foods
	A	
	A–	Muir Glen, Westbrae, Native Forest
B	**B+**	Natural Value, Santa Cruz Organic
	B	Progresso, Green Giant, Sunsweet, Tree Top, Ocean Spray
	B–	Mott's
C	**C+**	
	C	Oregon, Glory Foods
	C–	
D	**D+**	Del Monte, S&W, Contadina, Dole
	D	
	D–	Hunt's, French's
F	**F**	Libby's

CANNED FRUIT & VEGETABLES

WHAT YOU NEED TO KNOW

While "organic" has become increasingly popular in fresh produce sections of supermarkets, there is a small, but growing, selection of canned fruits and vegetables available on the aisle shelves.

GREEN HERO

Muir Glen

☆ First organic tomato processor in US
☆ Environmental leader in food industry
☆ GAM certified Green Business

CORPORATE VILLAIN

Libby's (Kraft)

☠ Greenwash Award for public deception
☠ Named global climate change laggard
☠ Undermines overseas health standards
☠ Paid $178* million to Washington lobbyists

RESOURCES

🖥 www.muirglen.com
🖥 www.edenfoods.com
🖥 www.scojuice.com

CARS

A	**A+**	
	A	
	A–	
B	**B+**	Toyota, Lexus, Scion
	B	Honda, Acura
	B–	
C	**C+**	Subaru
	C	Porsche, Hyundai, Kia, BMW, Audi, Renault, Peugeot, Volkswagen, Tata, Jaguar, Land Rover, Mercedes
	C–	Mini, Isuzu, Mazda, Smart Car
D	**D+**	Suzuki, Infiniti, Nissan
	D	Mitsubishi
	D–	
F	**F**	Chrysler, General Motors, Jeep, Dodge, Ford, Volvo, GMC, Lincoln, Mercury, Buick, Cadillac, Saturn, Chevrolet, Saab, Hummer

CARS

BUYING TIPS:
✓ Look for cars that get at least 30 MPG
✓ Think about a hybrid vehicle for your next car
✓ Consider buying carbon offsets for your car

CORPORATE VILLAIN

Chrysler

☠ UCS worst environmental auto ranking
☠ Paid $54 million to Washington lobbyists
☠ #53 of PERI 100 Most Toxic Air Polluters
☠ $12 billion paid by taxpayers to bailout

CORPORATE VILLAIN

General Motors

☠ Leader in fighting clean air legislation
☠ Paid $107 million to Washington lobbyists
☠ MM's "Worst Corporation" list for 4 years
☠ $31 billion paid by taxpayers to bailout

RESOURCES
🖥 www.fueleconomy.gov
🖥 www.betterworldclub.com
🖥 www.terrapass.com
🖥 www.toyota.com/prius

CELL PHONES & SERVICE

A	**A+**	Better World Telecom, Credo, Working Assets
	A	Earth Tones
	A–	
B	**B+**	Apple
	B	Sony, Nokia, Ericsson
	B–	AT&T
C	**C+**	Motorola
	C	STI Mobile, TracFone, MetroPCS, Jabra, Kyocera, Audiovox, Sanyo, BlackBerry, Palm, US Cellular, Cricket
	C–	
D	**D+**	T-Mobile, Sprint Nextel, Virgin, Boost Mobile
	D	Samsung, Siemens
	D–	Windows Mobile, LG, Acer
F	**F**	Verizon

CELL PHONES & SERVICE

WHAT YOU NEED TO KNOW

Cell phones are part of a billion dollar industry. Make sure that this significant revenue stream is going toward building a better world rather than tearing it apart.

BUYING TIPS

✓ Remember to recycle your old cell phone(s)
✓ Look for solar chargers to reduce energy use

GREEN HERO

Credo (Working Assets)

☆ Given $60 million to a range of nonprofits
☆ Purchases carbon offsets for energy use
☆ Educates for engaged citizenship

CORPORATE VILLAIN

Verizon

☠ Given $133 million to Washington lobbyists
☠ CEP "F" for overall social responsibility
☠ Discriminated against pregnant employees

RESOURCES

🖥 www.workingassets.com
🖥 www.earthtones.com
🖥 www.betterworldtelecom.com

CEREAL

A	**A+**	
	A	Alvarado Street, Nature's Path, Envirokidz, Barbara's
	A –	Peace Cereal, Arrowhead Mills, Health Valley, Earth's Best, Yogi
B	**B +**	Lundberg, Bob's Red Mill, Newman's Own, Food For Life, Cascadian Farm
	B	General Mills, Pillsbury, Wheaties, Nature Valley, Cheerios, Chex, Total, Quaker, Mother's, Kix
	B –	
C	**C +**	Kelloggs, Kashi, Corn Flakes, All-Bran, Frosted Flakes, Rice Crispies, Special K, Raisin Bran, Bear Naked
	C	Malt-O-Meal, Cream of Wheat, Weetabix
	C –	Weight Watchers, Heartland
D	**D +**	Post, Grape Nuts, Shredded Wheat
	D	
	D –	
F	**F**	Kraft, Nabisco, Back To Nature

CEREAL

WHAT YOU NEED TO KNOW
Currently, choosing a socially responsible
cereal is one of the easiest ways to make a
difference with your dollars. There are a wide
variety of excellent choices available in most
supermarkets.

GREEN HERO

Nature's Path

☆ GAM certified Green Business
☆ Named one of Canada's Greenest Employers
☆ Sponsors environmental efforts and festivals

CORPORATE VILLAIN

Back To Nature (Kraft)

☠ Part of #2 worst company on the earth
☠ MM's "Worst Corporation" list for 5 years
☠ Currently target of 2 major boycotts
☠ Named global climate change laggard

RESOURCES
🖥 www.peacecereal.com
🖥 www.barbarasbakery.com
🖥 www.envirokidz.com
🖥 www.naturespath.com

CHIPS

A	**A+**	
	A	Barbara's
	A–	Little Bear, Bearitos, Garden of Eatin', Hain, Terra, Kettle Chips
B	**B+**	Lundberg, Casa Sanchez
	B	Lay's, Cheetos, Doritos, Fritos, Sun Chips, Tostitos, Ruffles, Quaker, Funyuns
	B–	Pepperidge Farm
C	**C+**	
	C	True North, Cape Cod, Solea, Utz, Eat Smart, Stacy's, Boulder, Glicks, Genisoy, Guiltless Gourmet, Food Should Taste Good, Robert's, Dirty's, Hawaiian, Margaritaville, Mission
	C–	
D	**D+**	
	D	
	D–	French's, Alexia
F	**F**	Pringles, Nabisco

CHIPS

BUYING TIPS
✓ Look for chips made with organic ingredients
✓ Avoid hydrogenated, saturated and trans fats
✓ Buy larger quantities to reduce packaging

GREEN HERO

Kettle Chips

☆ 100% of waste oil turned into biodiesel
☆ Restored local wetlands habitat
☆ One of the largest solar arrays in NW
☆ Gives tons of potatoes to hunger orgs

CORPORATE VILLAIN

Nabisco (Kraft)

☠ Greenwash Award for public deception
☠ Continues to do business in Burma
☠ Named global climate change laggard
☠ Refuses to disclose data on diversity
☠ Spent over $178* million on lobbyists

RESOURCES
🖳 www.kettlefoods.com
🖳 www.barbarasbakery.com
🖳 www.lundberg.com

CHOCOLATE

A	**A+**	Endangered Species, Rapunzel, Equal Exchange, AlterEco, Divine
	A	Theo, Shaman, Terra Nostra, Sjaak's
	A–	Green & Black's, Dagoba
B	**B+**	Ah!Laska, Newman's Own, Cloud Nine, Tropical Source, Sunspire
	B	
	B–	
C	**C+**	
	C	Hershey's, Scharffen Berger, Droste, Godiva, Ferrero Rocher, Russell Stover, Lindt, Ritter, Valor, Nutella, Chocolove, Whitman's, Ghirardelli, Veritas, Ovaltine
	C–	
D	**D+**	
	D	Cadbury
	D–	Dove, Swiss Miss
F	**F**	Nestle, Perugina, Toblerone, Crunch

CHOCOLATE

WHAT YOU NEED TO KNOW
Recently, the ILO, UNICEF and US State Department uncovered the widespread use of child slave labor in the chocolate industry — up to 40% of all chocolate is currently being produced in this way.

BUYING TIPS
✓ Companies in the A category are slave-free
✓ Look for chocolate that is fair trade certified
✓ Buy organic chocolate when available

GREEN HERO

Endangered Species

☆ Ethically traded, organic, slave-free chocolate
☆ Suppliers = small, family-owned farms
☆ Eco-certified (LEED) production plant
☆ 10% of profits donated to wildlife groups

CORPORATE VILLAIN

Nestle

☠ "Most Irresponsible" corporation award
☠ Aggressive takeovers of family farms
☠ Involved in child slavery lawsuit
☠ Baby formula human rights boycott

CLEANING PRODUCTS

A	**A+**	Seventh Generation, Earth Friendly, Method, Dr. Bronner's, Oxo Brite
	A	Biokleen, Planet, Air Therapy, ECOS, Ecover, Citri-Glow, Citra-Solv
	A–	Mrs. Meyers, Shaklee
B	**B+**	LifeTree
	B	Bon Ami, Simple Green, 3M
	B–	Ajax, Colgate, Palmolive, Murphy Oil
C	**C+**	Pledge, SC Johnson, Drano, Vanish, Fantastik, Windex, Ziploc, Glade
	C	Hefty, Comet, WD-40
	C–	Amway, Sara Lee
D	**D+**	
	D	Arm & Hammer
	D–	Clorox, Green Works, Pine Sol, Tilex, SOS, Glad, Liquid-Plumr, 409, Lysol, Easy-Off, Wizard, Reckitt Benckiser, Chore Boy, Resolve, Woolite
F	**F**	Soft Scrub, Joy, Procter & Gamble, Ivory, Swiffer, Dial, Mr. Clean, Dawn

CLEANING PRODUCTS

BUYING TIPS
✓ Look for non-petroleum based products
✓ Avoid products with chlorine/toxic chemicals

GREEN HERO
Seventh Generation

☆ #1 best company on the planet
☆ Empowers consumers w/packaging
☆ Winner, Sustainability Report Award
☆ Socially Responsible Business Award

CORPORATE VILLAIN
Clorox

☠ On MM's "10 Worst Corporations" list
☠ Continues unnecessary animal testing
☠ Refuses disclosure to consumers
☠ Major producer of chlorine — dioxin

RESOURCES
🖥 www.seventhgeneration.com
🖥 www.ecover.com
🖥 www.drbronner.com

CLOTHING

A	**A +**	Patagonia, TS Designs, Autonomie
	A	No Enemy, Hempys, Ecolution, Deva, Maggie's Organics, Justice Clothing
	A –	Eileen Fisher, American Apparel
B	**B +**	Levi's, Liz Claiborne, Timberland
	B	Gap, Nordstrom, Cutter & Buck, LL Bean, Eddie Bauer, Coldwater Creek
	B –	Abercrombie & Fitch, H&M, J Crew, PVH, Bass, Izod, Calvin Klein
C	**C +**	Tommy Hilfiger, Nicole Miller, Burberry, Quiksilver, Rip Curl
	C	Men's Warehouse, The North Face
	C –	American Eagle
D	**D +**	Hanes, Champion, Beefy-T
	D	Target, Express, Limited, Victoria's Secret, Esprit, Bill Blass, Land's End, Fruit of the Loom, JC Penney
	D –	Russell, Guess, DKNY, Kohl's
F	**F**	Wal-Mart, Sam's Club, Macy's, Polo, Jones, Marshall Fields, Foley's, LA Gear, Dillard's, Disney, Kmart, TJ Maxx, Perry Ellis, Vanity Fair, Ralph Lauren, Marshall's, Consolidated

CLOTHING

WHAT YOU NEED TO KNOW

The fact is that many of the clothes we wear today are made in sweatshops in the developing world. Better companies have either US-made clothing or strictly enforced human rights standards that ensure fair wages and safe working conditions.

GREEN HERO

Autonomie Project

☆ Offers organic, sweatshop-free clothing
☆ Highest standard in the industry
☆ Includes eco-friendly, fair trade shoes
☆ GAM certified Green Business

CORPORATE VILLAIN

Macy's

☠ Weak code of conduct for sweatshops
☠ Refuses disclosure on its business
☠ Named "Sweatshop Laggard" by CEP
☠ "Bottom Rung", Ladder of Responsibility

RESOURCES

⌨ www.cleanclothes.org
⌨ www.americanapparel.net
⌨ www.autonomieproject.com
⌨ www.patagonia.com

COFFEE

A	**A+**	Thanksgiving, Cafe Humana, Equal Exchange
	A	Cafe Campesino, Café Mam, Elan, Pachamama, Peace Coffee, AlterEco, Newman's Own, Caffe Ibis, Grounds For Change, Larry's Beans, Higher Grounds, Alterra, Green Mountain
	A−	LOCAL COFFEE SHOPS
B	**B+**	Peet's
	B	
	B−	Starbucks, Seattle's Best
C	**C+**	
	C	Continental, Eight O'Clock, Hill Bros, MJB, Millstone, Folgers
	C−	illy, LaVazza
D	**D+**	
	D	International Delight
	D−	
F	**F**	Maxwell House, Gevalia, Sanka, General Foods, Yuban, Nescafe, Nestle, CoffeeMate

COFFEE

WHAT YOU NEED TO KNOW
Global coffee prices have plummeted recently, pushing some coffee farmers in the developing world to the brink of starvation. Buying fair trade coffee is now more important than ever.

BUYING TIPS
✓ Look for fair trade, shade grown, organic
✓ Support local, independent coffee shops

GREEN HERO
Thanksgiving Coffee

☆ Supports religious tolerance & wildlife
☆ Uses biodiesel trucks for transportation
☆ Fair trade, organic, shade grown coffee

CORPORATE VILLAIN
Nescafe (Nestle)

☠ Involved in union busting outside US
☠ "Bottom Rung", Ladder of Responsibility
☠ Aggressive takeovers of family farms
☠ Baby formula human rights boycott

RESOURCES
🖳 www.transfairusa.org
🖳 www.thanksgivingcoffee.com
🖳 www.equalexchange.com

COMPUTERS & ACCESSORIES

A	**A+**	
	A	GreenDisk
	A−	HP, Compaq
B	**B+**	Apple, IBM, Intel, Dell, Toshiba
	B	Sony, Canon, AMD, Sun, Lexmark
	B−	NEC, Adobe
C	**C+**	NCR, Micron, Motorola, Imation
	C	Panasonic, Oki, Brother, Asus, Best Buy, 3COM, Epson, Belkin, Creative, Kensington, Logitech, Plantronics, Sanyo, SanDisk, Fujitsu, Fellowes
	C−	Seagate, Sharp, Oracle, Maxell, LSI
D	**D+**	Philips, Samsung, JVC, Hitachi
	D	Viewsonic, Circuit City, CompUSA, Acer, Gateway, eMachines, Lenovo
	D−	LG
F	**F**	Microsoft, GE

COMPUTERS & ACCESSORIES

WHAT YOU NEED TO KNOW

Computers have become an essential part of everyday life for many of us, but that need to stay up-to-date has also led to a rapidly growing problem of toxic computer waste in our landfills.

GREEN HERO

HP (Hewlett Packard)

☆ Free return recycling of its computers
☆ Perfect 100 on HRC Equality Index
☆ Countless awards for business ethics

CORPORATE VILLAIN

Microsoft

☠ CEP "F" for overall social responsibility
☠ Named "abusive monopoly" by US Court
☠ Paid $89 million to Washington lobbyists
☠ Greenpeace "Green Electronics Laggard"
☠ Refuses disclosure on its business

RESOURCES

⌨ www.computertakeback.com
⌨ www.hp.com

CONDIMENTS

A	**A+**	Eden, Annie's
	A	Vegenaise, Sierra Nevada, San-J
	A−	Woodstock Farms, Spectrum, Muir Glen, Hain, Hollywood, Westbrae
B	**B+**	Ginger People, Nasoya, Organic Ville, Bragg's
	B	
	B−	
C	**C+**	Mrs. Dash
	C	Saffola, Lea & Perrins, Thai Kitchen, McCormick, Tabasco, Kikkoman, La Victoria, Tapatio
	C−	
D	**D+**	Del Monte, Contadina, Jack Daniel's, Heinz
	D	Lawry's, Best Foods, Lizano, Knorr
	D−	Hunt's, La Choy, Gulden's, KC Masterpiece, French's, Cattlemen's
F	**F**	Miracle Whip, Kraft, Bull's Eye, A1, Grey Poupon

CONDIMENTS

WHAT YOU NEED TO KNOW
Whether you're looking for ketchup, mustard, mayonnaise, barbeque sauce or soy sauce, there are now socially responsible brands of each.

BUYING TIPS
✓ Choose organic condiments when available

GREEN HERO
Sierra Nevada

☆ 98% of waste created is recycled
☆ Designated Climate Action Leader
☆ Numerous environmental awards
☆ Leader in eco-friendly brewing

CORPORATE VILLAIN
Miracle Whip (Kraft)

☠ Named "Top 10 Greenwasher"
☠ Involved in document deletion cover-up
☠ Continues to do business in Burma
☠ Paid $178* million to Washington lobbyists

RESOURCES
🖥 www.sierranevada.com
🖥 www.edenfoods.com
🖥 www.anniesinc.com

COOKIES & CRACKERS

A	**A+**	
	A	Mary's Gone Crackers, Barbara's, Natures Path, Annies, San-J, Lydia's
	A-	Alternative Baking Co, Sun Flour Baking Co, Nature's Choice, Hain, Immaculate, Health Valley, Doctor Kracker, Earth's Best, Late July, O'Cocos, Edward & Sons
B	**B+**	Newman's Own, Cascadian Farm, Lundberg
	B	Quaker, Mother's, Mi-del
	B-	Pepperidge Farm
C	**C+**	Keebler, Kashi, Famous Amos, Sunshine, Kellogg's
	C	Pamela's, LU, Archway, Loacker, Gille, Manishewitz, Ryvita, Wasa
	C-	
D	**D+**	Ry Krisp
	D	
	D-	Dove
F	**F**	Back To Nature, Snackwell's, Nabisco, Red Oval

COOKIES & CRACKERS

WHAT YOU NEED TO KNOW
The socially responsible cookie industry has recently exploded, so there's no longer any need to feel guilty about reaching into the cookie jar.

GREEN HERO

Newman's Own

☆ 100% of profits to education & charity
☆ CEP "A" for overall social responsibility
☆ Given over $200 million to good causes

CORPORATE VILLAIN

Nabisco (Kraft)

☠ Part of #2 worst company on the earth
☠ Currently the target of 2 major boycotts
☠ Spent over $178* million on lobbyists
☠ Greenwash Award for public deception

RESOURCES
🖳 www.newmansownorganics.com
🖳 www.barbarasbakery.com
🖳 www.annies.com
🖳 www.naturespath.com
🖳 www.healthvalley.com

COSMETICS

A	**A+**	
	A	Aveda, Aubrey, EO, Zia, Body Shop, Colorganics, Kiss My Face, Pangea
	A−	Dr. Hauschka, BWC, Lush
B	**B+**	Gabriel, Herbs of Grace, Ecco Bella, Zuzu, Grateful Body, Nature's Gate
	B	Avon, Desert Essence, Avalon
	B−	Johnson & Johnson, Aveeno, Neutrogena
C	**C+**	Physician's Formula
	C	La Cross, Sally Hansen, Wet & Wild, Burt's Bees, Cutex, Bare Escentuals
	C−	Estee Lauder
D	**D+**	Nivea, Revlon, Almay
	D	Dove, L'Oreal, Maybeline, Pond's, Chesebrough Ponds
	D−	
F	**F**	Max Factor, Olay, Covergirl

COSMETICS

WHAT YOU NEED TO KNOW

While some cosmetics companies still carry out tests on animals, many smaller companies now provide animal and eco-friendly alternatives.

BUYING TIPS

✓ Choose companies that don't test on animals
✓ Look for products with organic ingredients

GREEN HERO

Aveda

☆ Products never tested on animals
☆ Perfect score for social responsibility
☆ Sustainable sourcing of ingredients
☆ #5 best company on the planet

CORPORATE VILLAIN

CoverGirl (Proctor & Gamble)

☠ Continues unnecessary animal testing
☠ "Bottom Rung", Ladder of Responsibility
☠ MM's "10 Worst Corporations" list for 2 years
☠ Paid $38 million to Washington lobbyists

RESOURCES

🖥 www.aveda.com
🖥 www.caringconsumer.com

DAIRY ALTERNATIVES

A	**A+**	Organic Valley, Nancy's
	A	Stonyfield Farm, Wildwood, WholeSoy
	A−	So Delicious, Follow Your Heart, Purely Decadent, Soy/Rice Dream
B	**B+**	Good Karma
	B	Tofu/Vegan/Almond Rella, Soya Kaas, ZenSoy
	B−	
C	**C+**	
	C	Lisanatti, Tofutti, Soy Moon, Soyco, Soymage, Veggie/Rice Slice, Silk
	C−	Galaxy Nutritional
D	**D+**	
	D	International Delight
	D−	
F	**F**	Cool Whip, Carnation

DAIRY ALTERNATIVES

BUYING TIPS
✓ Choose organic products when available
✓ Look for items with easily recycled containers

GREEN HERO
Stonyfield Farm

☆ Actively reduces greenhouse gas emissions
☆ Awards for business ethics and integrity
☆ EPA "Green Partner Of The Year"

GREEN HERO
Nancy's

☆ Top rated for its organic integrity
☆ GAM certified Green Business
☆ Socially Responsible Business Award

CORPORATE VILLAIN
Cool Whip (Kraft)

☻ Named global climate change laggard
☻ Undermines overseas health standards
☻ #2 contributor to Washington lobbyists
☻ Continues to do business in Burma

DAIRY PRODUCTS

A	**A+**	Organic Valley, Nancy's
	A	Organic Pastures, Stonyfield Farm, Redwood Hill, Brown Cow, Straus
	A–	Wallaby, Helios
B	**B+**	Clover Stornetta, Lifeway
	B	Tillamook, Cabot, Yoplait
	B–	Lactaid, Dannon
C	**C+**	
	C	Sargento, Precious, Pavel's, Borden, Kozy Shack, Cascade Fresh, Crystal, Mountain High, President, Liberte, Rondele, Alouette, Athenos, Chavrie, Land O' Lakes, Rachel's, Kerrygold, Horizon, Alta Dena, Hood, Laughing Cow, Alpine Lace, Daisy
	C–	Weight Watchers, Sara Lee, Continental
D	**D+**	
	D	
	D–	Hunt's, Reddi-Wip
F	**F**	Jell-O, Kraft, Back to Nature, Nestle, Knudsen, Velveeta, Cracker Barrel, Philadephia Cream Cheese

DAIRY PRODUCTS

WHAT YOU NEED TO KNOW
While large corporate farms are the norm for the dairy industry, many small, family farms are fighting back by going organic in order to survive.

BUYING TIPS
✓ Look for "No Hormones" and "No Antibiotics"
✓ Choose items made with organic ingredients

GREEN HERO
Organic Valley

☆ Cooperative of small, family farms
☆ Top rated for its organic integrity
☆ Multiple responsible business awards

CORPORATE VILLAIN
Back to Nature (Kraft)

☠ Part of #2 worst company on the earth
☠ Currently the target of 2 major boycotts
☠ Greenwash Award for public deception

RESOURCES
🖥 www.cornucopia.org
🖥 www.organicvalley.coop
🖥 www.stonyfield.com

DENTAL CARE

A	**A+**	Preserve
	A	Kiss My Face, Tom's of Maine, Auromere,
	A–	Ecodent, NOW, Xyliwhite
B	**B+**	Radius, Natural Dentist, Jason, Nature's Gate, Fuchs
	B	Colgate, Ultra Brite, Desert Essence
	B–	ACT, Reach, Rembrandt, Efferdent, Johnson & Johnson, Listerine, Plax
C	**C+**	
	C	Burt's Bees, POH, GUM, Weleda, Orajel, Chattem
	C–	
D	**D+**	
	D	Arm & Hammer, Pepsodent, Aim, Mentadent
	D–	Aquafresh, Sensodyne, Polident, Poligrip, Abreva, GlaxoSmithKline
F	**F**	Scope, Oral-B, Crest, Fixodent, Anbesol, Procter & Gamble

DENTAL CARE

WHAT YOU NEED TO KNOW
Smaller, environmentally friendly companies now offer increasingly popular alternatives to the dental products of larger, mainstream corporations.

BUYING TIPS
✓ Look for products made with recycled content
✓ Buy items with easily recycled packaging

GREEN HERO
Preserve (Recycline)

☆ Environmental leader in industry
☆ Products from 100% recycled plastic
☆ Take-back recycling of all products

CORPORATE VILLAIN
Crest (Proctor & Gamble)

☠ GAM "Bottom Rung", Ladder of Responsibility
☠ WWF named "environmental laggard"
☠ Paid $38 million to Washington lobbyists

RESOURCES
🖥 www.recycline.com
🖥 www.tomsofmaine.com

DESSERTS

A	**A+**	
	A	Amy's Kitchen
	A–	
B	**B+**	Wholly Wholesome, Vermont Mystic Pie Co, Tru Whip, Ah!Laska
	B	Cabot, Pillsbury, Yoplait
	B–	Pepperidge Farm
C	**C+**	
	C	Mrs. Smith's, Mrs. Field's, Duncan Hines, Dr. Oetker, Claim Jumper
	C–	Sara Lee, Weight Watchers
D	**D+**	
	D	
	D–	Marie Callender's, Reddi-wip
F	**F**	Kraft, Cool Whip, Jell-O

DESSERTS

WHAT YOU NEED TO KNOW

If you don't have time to bake your own pie from the apple tree in your back yard, your best option is to buy an organic apple pie from the store.

BUYING TIPS

✓ Look for items made with organic ingredients

GREEN HERO

Amy's Kitchen

☆ Donates food to relief efforts
☆ Produces all-vegetarian, organic foods
☆ GAM certified Green Business

CORPORATE VILLAIN

Jell-O (Kraft)

☠ Named "Top 10 Greenwasher"
☠ Involved in document deletion cover-up
☠ Continues to do business in Burma
☠ Currently the target of 2 major boycotts
☠ Paid $178* million to Washington lobbyists

RESOURCES

🖥 www.amyskitchen.com
🖥 www.whollywholesome.com

EGGS

A	**A+**	Organic Valley
	A	
	A –	Humane Harvest, Veg-a-Fed, Chino Valley, Pete & Gerry's, Judy's Family Farm, Mother's
B	**B+**	Clover Stornetta, Born Free
	B	Eggland's Best
	B –	
C	**C+**	Rock Island
	C	Gold Circle Farms, Land O'Lakes, Second Nature, Horizon Organic, Eggology
	C –	Nulaid, Decoster
D	**D+**	Lucerne
	D	
	D –	Egg Beaters
F	**F**	

EGGS

WHAT YOU NEED TO KNOW
Factory farming has made egg production today a cruel and environmentally damaging endeavor. Seek out smaller, more humane options.

BUYING TIPS
✓ Look for cage-free or free-range eggs
✓ Buy organic eggs whenever possible
✓ Seek out recycled paper-based packaging

GREEN HERO

Organic Valley

☆ Small, family farmer-owned cooperative
☆ Gives 10% of profits to local community
☆ Humane animal treatment a priority

CORPORATE VILLAIN

EggBeaters (ConAgra)

☠ Involved in major accounting scandal
☠ 2nd largest E. coli meat recall in history
☠ Many worker safety & health violations

RESOURCES
🖳 www.organicvalley.coop

ELECTRONICS

A	A+	
	A	
	A–	
B	B+	Apple, Toshiba, Kodak
	B	Sony, Aiwa, Texas Instruments, 3M, Canon
	B–	
C	C+	Conair, Norelco, Minolta, Konica, Denon, Polaroid
	C	Panasonic, Sharp, TDK, Haier, Apex, Magnavox, Eveready, Best Buy, Fuji, Kenwood, Grundig, Pentax, Sanyo, Koss, Energizer, Garmin, Sylvania, Plantronics, Nikon, Tivo, Rayovac, Sennheiser, Coby, Uniden, Olympus
	C–	Fry's, RCA, Thomson, Maxell
D	D+	Hitachi, Samsung, Emerson, Delphi, Philips, Bosch, JVC, Vizio, Viewsonic
	D	Radio Shack, Mitsubishi, Amazon
	D–	LG, Goldstar
F	F	GE (General Electric), Duracell, Daewoo, Microsoft, Nintendo

ELECTRONICS

WHAT YOU NEED TO KNOW
Our addiction to the latest electronics has created a significant drain on our energy grid (even when they're off!) as well as a major recycling problem.

BUYING TIPS
✓ Look for electronics with Energy Star labels
✓ Buy rechargeable (NiMH) batteries
✓ Choose electronics that are recyclable

GREEN HERO

Apple

☆ Takes back iPods & computers for recycling
☆ All computers are Energy Star certified
☆ Perfect 100 on HRC Equality Index for 7 years

CORPORATE VILLAIN

GE (General Electric)

☠ Major producer of landmines and weapons
☠ Creator of 5 Superfund sites
☠ Target of environmental boycott
☠ Paid $196 million to Washington lobbyists

RESOURCES
🖥 www.apple.com/environment
🖥 www.sony.net/SonyInfo/csr

ENERGY BARS

A	**A+**	CLIF, Luna, Alpsnack
	A	BumbleBar, Nutiva, Nature's Path, Optimum
	A−	ReBar, Raw Revolution, Larabar, Health Valley, Think, Boomi, ProBar,
B	**B+**	Kind, Crispy Cat, Cascadian Farm
	B	Quaker, Nature Valley, General Mills
	B−	
C	**C+**	Kellogg's, Kashi, Nutrigrain
	C	Atkins, Roman Meal, Tiger's Milk, Soy Joy, Fit Smart, Promax, Met-Rx, Odwalla, Genisoy, Fubar, Sunbelt
	C−	
D	**D+**	
	D	
	D−	Slim Fast, Zone, Kudos, Snickers
F	**F**	Balance, South Beach, PowerBar

ENERGY BARS

WHAT YOU NEED TO KNOW
Because many energy bar companies have truly stepped up to the plate, your choice of energy bar is one of the easiest ways to make a powerful difference for people and the planet.

GREEN HERO
CLIF

☆ #4 best company on the earth
☆ Winner, Business Ethics Award
☆ EPA Green Power Leader award winner

CORPORATE VILLAIN
Balance (Kraft)

☠ Part of #2 worst company on the earth
☠ Named global climate change laggard
☠ Undermines overseas health standards
☠ #2 contributor to Washington lobbyists

RESOURCES
🖥 www.clifbar.com
🖥 www.alpsnack.com
🖥 www.bumblebar.com
🖥 www.nutiva.com

ENERGY DRINKS

A	**A+**	Guayaki, Honest Tea, CLIF, Adina
	A	Steaz, Zola, Sambazon
	A−	Bossa Nova, Kaboom
B	**B+**	Monster, Hansen's, Blue Sky, Recharge, Jones
	B	AMP, MDX, Gatorade, SoBe, Propel, No Fear
	B−	Starbucks, Snapple
C	**C+**	Special K
	C	5-Hour Energy, FRS, Red Bull, Rip It, Bawls, Atkins, Arizona, Rockstar, Go, Girl, Muscle Milk, Guru, Fubar, Everlast, Celsius, Met-Rx, Xenergy
	C−	
D	**D+**	
	D	180, Lipton
	D−	Ensure, Boost, Slim Fast
F	**F**	Fuze, Vitamin Water, Full Throttle, BPM, Powerade, Vault, Glaceau, Tab

ENERGY DRINKS

WHAT YOU NEED TO KNOW
Just in the last 2 years have socially responsible choices for energy drinks finally become available. Its important to support these options wherever you find them.

BUYING TIPS
✓ Buy drinks in aluminum or glass containers

GREEN HERO
Guayaki

☆ Organic, fair trade certified products
☆ Uses sustainably harvested, rainforest plants
☆ 3x Awarded "Most Democratic Workplace"
☆ GAM certified Green Business

CORPORATE VILLAIN
Full Throttle (Coca Cola)

☠ MM's "Worst Corporation" list for 3 years
☠ Hinders clean water access abroad
☠ Target of major human rights boycotts

RESOURCES
⌨ www.guayaki.com
⌨ www.steaz.com
⌨ www.stopcorporateabuse.org

FAST FOOD & CASUAL DINING

A	**A+**	
	A	Chipotle, Burgerville, Pizza Fusion, Evos, Boloco, Organic To Go
	A–	
B	**B+**	Bruegger's Bagels, Einstein Bros.
	B	Panera, In-N-Out, Noodles & Co
	B–	
C	**C+**	Subway
	C	Church's Chicken, Dunkin Donuts, Togo's, Blimpie, Chuck E Cheese, Ruby Tuesdays, Applebee's
	C–	Chik-fil-A, DQ, IHOP, Little Caesar's, Macaroni Grill, Outback Steakhouse, Panda Express, Papa John's, Olive Garden, Popeye's, Qdoba, Quiznos, Red Robin, Red Lobster, Sizzler's
D	**D+**	Carl's Jr., Hardee's, Sonic, Denny's
	D	Burger King, Jack in the Box, TGI Fridays, Arby's, Cracker Barrel
	D–	McDonald's, Wendy's, Domino's
F	**F**	KFC, Taco Bell, Baja Fresh, A&W, Pizza Hut, Long John Silver

FAST FOOD & CASUAL DINING

WHAT YOU NEED TO KNOW

The overall picture of the highly competitive fast food industry is not a pretty one, but if you find yourself in a pinch, there are a handful of companies to choose from that are on the cutting edge of responsibility. Support them whenever possible and let them know that you appreciate their efforts.

GREEN HERO

Chipotle

☆ Actively sources from family farms
☆ 30% of beans utilized are organic
☆ 50-100% of meat utilized is natural-raised

CORPORATE VILLAIN

KFC (Kentucky Fried Chicken)

☒ Linked to rainforest destruction abroad
☒ Involved with plastic toy sweatshops
☒ Target of major consumer boycott
☒ Evidence of false nutritional claims

RESOURCES

🖥 www.chipotle.com
🖥 www.burgerville.com

FEMININE CARE

A	**A+**	Seventh Generation
	A	Keeper, Diva Cup, Gladrags
	A–	Maxim, Organic Essentials, Natracare
B	**B+**	
	B	Kotex, Poise
	B–	EPT, Stayfree, O.B., Clear Blue Easy, Carefree
C	**C+**	
	C	Playtex, Vagisil, Summer's Eve
	C–	
D	**D+**	
	D	First Response
	D–	Massengil
F	**F**	Always, Tampax

FEMININE CARE

WHAT YOU NEED TO KNOW
Much of the effort for socially responsible business has been driven by women, so it's not surprising that there are many great options in this category.

BUYING TIPS
✓ Buy care products with less packaging waste

GREEN HERO

Seventh Generation

☆ Ranked #1 best company on the planet
☆ Empowers consumers w/packaging
☆ Socially Responsible Business Award

CORPORATE VILLAIN

Tampax (P&G)

☻ MM's "Worst Corporation" list for 2 years
☻ Continues unnecessary animal testing
☻ Target of major consumer boycott

RESOURCES
🖥 www.gladrags.com
🖥 www.keeper.com
🖥 www.seventhgen.com
🖥 www.divacup.com

FROZEN DINNERS

A	**A+**	
	A	Amy's Kitchen
	A–	Rising Moon, Moosewood, Applegate Farms, Cedarlane, Seeds of Change, Ethnic Gourmet, Organic Classics
B	**B+**	Cascadian Farm, Linda McCartney
	B	Ian's, Totino's
	B–	
C	**C+**	Kashi
	C	Birds Eye, Swanson, Hungry Man, Foster Farms, Michelina's, Tina's, Red Baron, Claim Jumper, Michael Angelo's, Gorton's, Van de Kamps, Health Is Wealth, Ling Ling, White Castle, Lean Gourmet
	C–	Quorn, Weight Watchers, Bravissimo
D	**D+**	TGI Friday's, Ore-Ida, Smart Ones, Boston Market, Bagel Bites
	D	Bertolli
	D–	Uncle Ben's, Healthy Choice, Marie Callendar's, Banquet, Alexia
F	**F**	Stouffer's, Lean Cuisine, Tyson, South Beach, Hot Pockets, Boca

FROZEN DINNERS

WHAT YOU NEED TO KNOW
Today's stress-filled lifestyles have created increasing demand for quick and easy meals. Luckily, a number of responsible companies have decided to focus on options that are good for people and the planet.

GREEN HERO

Amy's Kitchen

☆ Donates food to relief efforts
☆ Produces all-vegetarian, organic foods
☆ GAM certified Green Business

CORPORATE VILLAIN

Stouffer's (Nestle)

☠ Aggressive takeovers of family farms
☠ Baby formula human rights boycott
☠ "Most Irresponsible" corporation award
☠ Involved in union busting outside US

RESOURCES
🖥 www.amyskitchen.com
🖥 www.fairfieldfarmkitchens.com
🖥 www.risingmoon.com
🖥 www.seedsofchange.com

FRUIT & VEGETABLES

	A+	FARMERS MARKETS, CSAs
A	A	Earthbound Farm, Sunridge Farms
	A–	Stahlbush, Cal-Organic, Bunny Luv, Woodstock Farms, Made In Nature, Grimmway Farms, Sunview, Sno Pac
B	B+	Cascadian Farm, Newman's Own, HerbThyme, Pure Pacific
	B	Green Giant, Driscoll's, Sunsweet, Ocean Spray, Sun-Maid, Tropicana, Ian's, Sunkist
	B–	
C	C+	Birds Eye, C&W
	C	Ready Pac, Salad Time, Flav-R-Pac, Christopher Ranch
	C–	
D	D+	Dole, Ore-Ida, Del Monte
	D	
	D–	Alexia, Hidden Valley
F	F	Fresh Express

FRUIT & VEGETABLES

WHAT YOU NEED TO KNOW
Fresh produce is the vanguard of the organic foods movement. It's particularly important to buy local produce, so attend your local farmers' market or join a CSA (community supported agriculture) farm.

BUYING TIPS
✓ Buy organic, locally grown produce

GREEN HERO

Earthbound Farm

☆ GAM certified Green Business
☆ Social Venture Network member
☆ Provide of 100% organic produce

CORPORATE VILLAIN

Fresh Express (Chiquita)

☠ MM's "Worst Corporation" list for 2 years
☠ Hired Columbian criminals to protect crops
☠ EC overall responsibility rating of POOR
☠ Evaded taxes using offshore bank accounts

RESOURCES
⌨ www.localharvest.org

GASOLINE

A	A+	
	A	
	A–	
B	B+	Sunoco
	B	
	B–	Hess
C	C+	Petro Canada
	C	Costco, Flying J, 7-Eleven, Jet, Husky, Mohawk, Sinclair, Circle K, Gulf
	C–	Citgo, Total, Valero, Diamond Shamrock, Beacon, Ultramar
D	D+	Marathon, Speedway, SuperAmerica, Ashland
	D	
	D–	BP, Amoco, Arco, Shell
F	F	Exxon, Mobil, Esso, Chevron, Texaco, Unocal, Conoco, Phillips 66, Tosco, Union 76

GASOLINE

WHAT YOU NEED TO KNOW
The petroleum industry is one of the least socially and environmentally responsible on the planet, so if you don't want to get your hands dirty, you should sell your car. For the rest of us, it's very important to avoid the companies at the bottom of this category as they are some of the most destructive in existence.

BUYING TIPS
✓ Locate the best ranked gas station near your home and work

GREEN HERO

Sunoco

☆ Most eco-friendly refineries in industry
☆ Only oil signatory to CERES Principles
☆ 1st company to recognize global warming

CORPORATE VILLAIN

Exxon-Mobil

☗ #1 worst corporation on the planet
☗ Renowned human rights violator
☗ #5 in "Top 100 Corporate Criminals"
☗ Paid $139 million to Washington lobbyists

HAIR CARE

A	**A+**	Druide
	A	Aveda, Tom's of Maine, EO, Aubrey Organics, Kiss My Face, Body Shop
	A−	Lush
B	**B+**	Nature's Gate, Ecco Bella, Jason, Alba, Pure & Basic, Giovanni, Shikai, Paul Mitchell, Pure Essentials, Abba
	B	Avalon, Desert Essence, Emerald Forest, Aloe Vera 80, BWC
	B−	Neutrogena, Aveeno
C	**C+**	VO5, Nexxus, St. Ives, Tresemme
	C	Citre Shine, Dep, L.A. Looks, Biosilk, AquaNet, Prell, Selsun Blue, Burt's Bees, Matrix, Joico, Biolage, Crew
	C−	
D	**D+**	Revlon
	D	L'Oréal, SunSilk, White Rain, Dove, Suave, Finesse, Axe
	D−	
F	**F**	Head & Shoulders, Herbal Essences, Pert, Pantene, Clairol, Aussie, Flex, Infusium, Revlon, Rogaine

HAIR CARE

BUYING TIPS
✓ Avoid products tested on animals
✓ Seek out items made with organic ingredients
✓ Look for recyclable containers — #1, #2 plastic
✓ Buy larger quantities to reduce packaging

GREEN HERO

Druide

☆ 100% sustainably harvested ingredients
☆ Uses strict ECOCERT organic standards
☆ Fair trade, organic ingredients
☆ Industry leader in environment category

CORPORATE VILLAIN

Clairol (Proctor & Gamble)

☠ Paid $38 million to Washington lobbyists
☠ MM's "Worst Corporation" list for 2 years
☠ Continues unnecessary animal testing

RESOURCES
🖳 www.druide.ca
🖳 www.aveda.com
🖳 www.thebodyshop.com
🖳 www.aubrey-organics.com

HOTELS

A	**A+**	
	A	Kimpton Hotels
	A–	
B	**B+**	Marriott, Courtyard, Ritz Carlton, Renaissance
	B	
	B–	Motel 6, Novotel, Sofitel
C	**C+**	Harrah's
	C	Comfort Inn, Comfort Suites, Quality Inn, Econolodge, Days Inn, Super 8, Ramada, Howard Johnson, Hyatt, Best Western, Holiday Inn, Travelodge, Radisson
	C–	Carlson
D	**D+**	Hilton, Hampton Inn, Doubletree, Embassy Suites
	D	Sheraton, Westin
	D–	
F	**F**	

HOTELS

WHAT YOU NEED TO KNOW
Whether for business or pleasure, choosing where you stay can have a greater impact than even how you travel there and back.

BUYING TIPS
✓ Whenever possible, stay in a locally-owned inn, bed & breakfast, or international hostel.

GREEN HERO

Kimpton Hotels

☆ Environmental leader in the hotel industry
☆ Perfect 100 on HRC Equality Index
☆ Green Seal certified green lodging
☆ CAM certified Green Business

CORPORATE VILLAIN

Sheraton (Starwood)

☠ CERES "Climate Change Laggard"
☠ Refuses disclosure to consumers
☠ CEP "F" for overall social responsibility

RESOURCES
🖥 www.environmentallyfriendlyhotels.com
🖥 www.travelocity.com/greentravel

ICE CREAM & FROZEN DESSERTS

A	**A+**	
	A	Ben & Jerry's, Sambazon, Wholesoy, Purely Decadent, Stonyfield Farm
	A−	So Delicious, Rice/Soy Dream, Julie's, Natural Choice, Humboldt Creamery, Alden's, Green & Black's
B	**B+**	Reed's, Newman's Own, FrutStix
	B	
	B−	Starbucks
C	**C+**	
	C	Tofutti, Crystal, Fruitfull, It's-It, Godiva, Choco's, Hershey's, Hood, Häagen Dazs, Ciao Bella
	C−	Weight Watchers
D	**D+**	Dole
	D	Breyers, Klondike, Good Humor, Frusen Gladje
	D−	Healthy Choice, Dove, Snickers
F	**F**	Dreyer's, Edy's, Nestle, Skinny Cow, Eskimo Pie

ICE CREAM & FROZEN DESSERTS

BUYING TIPS
✓ Choose ice cream with organic ingredients
✓ Look for fair trade coffee/chocolate flavors

GREEN HERO

Ben & Jerry's

☆ Socially responsible business leader
☆ Winner, Sustainability Report Award
☆ CEP "A" for overall social responsibility

CORPORATE VILLAIN

Dreyer's (Nestle)

☠ Baby formula human rights boycott
☠ "Most Irresponsible" corporation award
☠ Involved in child slavery lawsuit
☠ Aggressive takeovers of family farms

RESOURCES
🖥 www.benjerry.com
🖥 www.soydelicious.com
🖥 www.stonyfield.com
🖥 www.strausfamilycreamery.com

INSURANCE COMPANIES

A	**A+**	Better World Club
	A	
	A–	
B	**B+**	
	B	Travelers, Allstate
	B–	Chubb, TIAA-CREF, Nationwide, Cigna
C	**C+**	Progressive, Aetna, Pacific Life, Kaiser Permanente, Esurance, UnumProvident, Principal Financial
	C	Safeco, Mutual of Omaha, MetLife, State Farm, USAA, Amica, Humana, Libery Mutual, GEICO, MassMutual, New York Life, AAA
	C–	Prudential
D	**D+**	Northwestern Mutual, Capital One
	D	AFLAC
	D–	Blue Cross / Blue Shield
F	**F**	AIG

INSURANCE COMPANIES

WHAT YOU NEED TO KNOW
Whether for your car, health, home or life, most of us need to buy insurance sooner or later. As we've discovered with the recent corporate bailouts, who we choose to do business with can have serious implications for our personal and national pocketbooks.

GREEN HERO
Better World Club

☆ Social Venture Network member
☆ CAM certified Green Business
☆ Only insurance signatory to CERES Principles

CORPORATE VILLAIN
AIG (American International Group)

☠ MM's "Worst Corporation" list for 2 years
☠ Rated "Very Poor" by Ethical Consumer
☠ Paid $78 million to Washington lobbyists
☠ $170 billion paid by taxpayers to bailout

RESOURCES
🖳 www.betterworldclub.com
🖳 www.jdpower.com/insurance

JUICE

A	**A+**	Organic Valley, Adina
	A	Sambazon, Zola
	A−	Santa Cruz Organic, Bossa Nova, Purity, Lakewood, Apple & Eve, Columbia Gorge, Ginger People
B	**B+**	Cascadian Farm, Sonoma Sparkler, Hansen's, Mountain Sun, Newman's Own, RW Knudsen, After the Fall
	B	Naked Juice, Tropicana, Gatorade, Sunkist, Ocean Spray, TreeTop
	B−	V8, Hawaiian Punch, Snapple, ReaLemon, Campbell's, Mott's
C	**C+**	
	C	Welch's, Kern's, L&A, Ceres, POM, Martinelli's, Odwalla, Sunny D, Horizon Organic, Florida's Natural
	C−	
D	**D+**	Del Monte, Dole
	D	
	D−	
F	**F**	Capri Sun, Kool-Aid, Libby's, Crystal Light, Minute Maid, Simply Orange, Juicy Juice, Back to Nature

JUICE

BUYING TIPS
✓ Purchase organic juices when available
✓ Buy juices in aluminum or glass containers
✓ #1 or #2 when plastics are the only option
✓ Buy larger quantities to reduce packaging

GREEN HERO

Organic Valley

☆ Small family farmer-owned co-operative
☆ Gives 10% of profits to local community
☆ Humane animal treatment a priority
☆ Ranked #4 best company on the planet

CORPORATE VILLAIN

Minute Maid (Coca Cola)

☠ MM's "Worst Corporation" list for 3 years
☠ Hinders clean water access abroad
☠ Target of major human rights boycotts

RESOURCES
🖳 www.adinaworld.com
🖳 www.organicvalley.coop
🖳 www.newmansown.com

LAUNDRY SUPPLIES

A	**A+**	Seventh Generation, Earth Friendly, Oxo Brite, Method
	A	Biokleen, Planet, Ecover, ECOS
	A–	Country Save, Mountain Green, Oasis, Bio Pac, Shaklee, Mrs. Meyers
B	**B+**	Lifetree, Natural Value, Environne
	B	Fab, Fresh Start, Dynamo, Suavitel
	B–	
C	**C+**	Shout, Static Guard
	C	Sun Burst, Cuddle Soft, Spot Shot, All
	C–	
D	**D+**	
	D	Arm & Hammer, Oxi Clean, Xtra, Wisk, Surf, Snuggle
	D–	Clorox, Woolite, Calgon, Cling Free, Spray'n Wash, Vivid
F	**F**	20 Mule Team Borax, Purex, Biz, Bold, Downy, Tide, Bounce, Era, Gain, Ivory, Febreze, Cheer

LAUNDRY SUPPLIES

BUYING TIPS
✓ Avoid #3 plastic containers — choose #1 or #2
✓ Avoid phosphates and chlorine bleach

GREEN HERO

Ecover

☆ GAM certified Green Business
☆ Winner, environmental leader award
☆ UN Global 500 Environment Honor Roll
☆ 1st truly ecological factory in the world

CORPORATE VILLAIN

Clorox

☠ On MM's "10 Worst Corporations" list
☠ Continues unnecessary animal testing
☠ Refuses disclosure to consumers
☠ Major producer of chlorine — dioxin

RESOURCES
🖥 www.seventhgen.com
🖥 www.ecover.com
🖥 www.ecos.com
🖥 www.planetinc.com
🖥 www.biokleenhome.com

MEAT ALTERNATIVES

A	**A+**	
	A	Amy's, Fantastic Foods, Wildwood, Sunshine Burgers, Local Tofu
	A–	Yves, Small Planet, Turtle Island, Tofurkey, SoyBoy, FarmSoy, Unisoy, Vermont Soy, TofuTown
B	**B+**	Nasoya
	B	Ian's
	B–	Pete's Tofu, Vitasoy
C	**C+**	Morningstar Farms, Gardenburger
	C	Veggie Patch, Sweet Earth, Mori-Nu, Primal Strips, Health Is Wealth, Soy Deli, White Wave, Veat
	C–	Quorn
D	**D+**	
	D	
	D–	Lightlife
F	**F**	Boca

MEAT ALTERNATIVES

WHAT YOU NEED TO KNOW

Meat alternatives have come a long way since the days of tofu jokes. Burgers, hot dogs, chicken strips, lunch meat, and more are now convincingly tasty in vegetarian form and tend to have a smaller ecological footprint than their counterparts.

GREEN HERO

Amy's Kitchen

☆ Produces all-vegetarian, organic foods
☆ GAM certified Green Business
☆ Donates food to relief efforts

CORPORATE VILLAIN

Boca (Kraft)

☠ MM's "Worst Corporation" list for 5 years
☠ Greenwash Award for public deception
☠ Spent over $178* million on lobbyists

RESOURCES

🖥 www.amyskitchen.com
🖥 www.tofurkey.com

MEAT PRODUCTS

A	**A+**	Organic Prairie
	A	Lindner Bison, Green Zabiha
	A–	Shelton's, MBA Brand, Coleman, Niman Ranch, Diestel, Applegate Farms, Five Dot Ranch, Eel River
B	**B+**	
	B	
	B–	
C	**C+**	
	C	Foster Farms, Valley Fresh, Saag's, Hickory Farms, Armour, Empire Kosher, Underwood, Thumann's
	C–	Hillshire Farm, Ball Park Franks, Jimmy Dean, Sara Lee
D	**D+**	Perdue, Hormel, Farmer John, SPAM, Jennie-O, Stagg
	D	
	D–	Banquet, Libby's, Hebrew National, Slim Jim, Healthy Choice
F	**F**	Oscar Mayer, Louis Rich, Tyson, Smithfield, Butterball, Farmland, Eckrich, Premium Standard, Cook's

MEAT PRODUCTS

WHAT YOU NEED TO KNOW
Meat production tends to consume more resources than agriculture, so it's especially important to choose sustainable, humane options.

BUYING TIPS
✓ Choose free-range, organic meat options

GREEN HERO
Organic Prairie (Organic Valley)

☆ Small, family farmer cooperative
☆ Gives 10% of profits to local community
☆ Humane animal treatment a priority

CORPORATE VILLAIN
Tyson Foods

☠ MM's "Worst Corporation" list for 2 years
☠ CEP "F" for overall social responsibility
☠ Guilty of 20+ violations of Clean Air Act

RESOURCES
🖥 www.organicprairie.com
🖥 www.smartchicken.com
🖥 www.colemannatural.com

MEDICAL

A	A+	Traditional Medicinals
	A	
	A−	Nature's Way
B	B+	Ricola
	B	3M
	B−	Johnson & Johnson, McNeil, Band-Aid, Rolaids, Neosporin, Visine, K-Y, Benadryl, Tylenol, Bengay, Motrin
C	C+	Novartis, Bausch & Lomb, TheraFlu, Genentech, Bristol-Myers Squibb
	C	Merck, Cortizone, Unisom, Insight, Chattem, Kaopectate, Del Pharma
	C−	
D	D+	Schering-Plough, Claritin, Dr. Scholl
	D	Halls, Cadbury Adams, Unilever, Q-Tips, Vaseline
	D−	Bayer, Abbott, Tums, Alka-Seltzer, Reckitt Benckiser, GlaxoSmithKline
F	F	Procter & Gamble, Wyeth, Roche, Pfizer, Pharmacia, Pepto-Bismol, Metamucil, Robitussin, Whitehall-Robins, Day/Nyquil, Advil, Vicks

MEDICAL

WHAT YOU NEED TO KNOW
Pharmaceutical companies are some of the most powerful and least responsible of any on the planet. When you do have a choice of medical products, it is very important that you choose the better companies.

BUYING TIPS
✓ Make sure to look on the back of the box to see what company manufactures an item

GREEN HERO
Traditional Medicinals
☆ GAM certified Green Business
☆ Powered by 100% renewable energy
☆ Utilizes sustainable harvesting of wild herbs
☆ Organic, fair trade, biodynamic ingredients

CORPORATE VILLAIN
Pfizer
☠ MM's "Worst Corporation" list for 5 years
☠ Named "Environmental Laggard" by CEP
☠ #17 in "Top 100 Corporate Criminals"
☠ Spent $93 million on Washington lobbyists

MILK & ALTERNATIVES

A	**A+**	Eden, Organic Valley, Nancy's
	A	Organic Pastures, Stonyfield Farm, Wildwood, Hemp Bliss, Straus
	A−	WestSoy, Soy Slender, Rice/Soy Dream, Helios
B	**B+**	AmaZake, Lifeway, Clover Stornetta, Living Harvest, Pacific Natural, Smart Balance
	B	Zensoy, Almond Breeze
	B−	Vitasoy, Lactaid
C	**C+**	
	C	Crystal, Land-O-Lakes, Kikkoman, Milkman, Horizon Organic, Silk, 8th Continent, The Organic Cow, Hood
	C−	
D	**D+**	
	D	Borden, Garelick, Meadow Gold, Berkeley Farms, Alta Dena, Mayfield
	D−	
F	**F**	Knudsen, Nestle

MILK & ALTERNATIVES

WHAT YOU NEED TO KNOW

Now there are a wide range of socially responsible options for both dairy and non-dairy milk lovers.

GREEN HERO

Organic Valley

☆ Ranked #3 best company on the planet
☆ Small family farmer-owned co-operative
☆ Humane animal treatment a priority
☆ Gives 10% of profits to local community

GREEN HERO

Straus Family

☆ 1ˢᵗ 100% organic dairy in US
☆ Uses returnable glass bottles for milk
☆ Utilizes methane capture for waste
☆ Small, sustainable family farm

RESOURCES

🖳 www.organicvalley.coop
🖳 www.strausmilk.com
🖳 www.edenfoods.com
🖳 www.cornucopia.org

OFFICE SUPPLIES

A	**A+**	
	A	
	A–	HP
B	**B+**	Herman Miller, Xerox, IBM
	B	Staples, Pitney Bowes, Ricoh, Canon
	B–	3M, Scotch, Post-it
C	**C+**	Imation, DHL, Crayola, Hallmark
	C	FedEx, Kinko's, Zebra, UPS, Fiskars, Elmer's, Sharpie, Sanford, Olympus, Pentel, Papermate, Uniball, Henkel, Parker, Duck, Ikon, Epson, Brother, Expo, Fellowes, Rubbermaid, Pilot, Kensington, Smead, Safco, Stanley
	C–	Airborne Express, Office Depot
D	**D+**	Bic, Sheaffer, BASF
	D	Avery, OfficeMax
	D–	Smurfit-Stone Container
F	**F**	Mead, At-A-Glance, Day Runner, Cambridge, Columbian, Five Star

OFFICE SUPPLIES

WHAT YOU NEED TO KNOW

Many of the items we use during the day are in some way related to our workplace. If you have any potential influence over office purchasing, consider suggesting a shift in funds over to more socially responsible products.

GREEN HERO

Herman Miller

☆ 100 Most Ethical Companies list, 7 years
☆ Business Ethics Award, 2 time winner
☆ Perfect 100 on HRC Equality Index
☆ Winner of Social Capitalist Award for ethics

CORPORATE VILLAIN

Mead (MeadWestvaco)

☠ Named global climate change laggard
☠ Continues unnecessary animal testing
☠ Refuses disclosure to consumers
☠ CEP "F" for overall social responsibility

RESOURCES

🖥 www.hp.com
🖥 www.ibm.com
🖥 www.hermanmiller.com

OIL, VINEGAR, OLIVES & PICKLES

A	**A+**	Eden Foods, Annie's, Rapunzel, Canaan Fair Trade, AlterEco
	A	Nutiva
	A−	Napa Valley Naturals, Spectrum, Hollywood, Mediterranean Organic, Hain, Bionaturae, NOW Foods
B	**B+**	Natural Value, Marukan, Republic of Tea, Newman's Own, Earth Balance, Cascadian Farm, Santa Barbara, Bragg
	B	
	B−	
C	**C+**	
	C	Star, Canola Harvest, Saffola, Sagra, Nakano, Mezzetta, Mt. Olive, Vlasic, Lindsay, Minasso, Armstrong, B&G, Cains, Bertolli, Nathan's, Crisco
	C−	
D	**D+**	Heinz, Del Monte
	D	Mazola
	D−	Wesson, Pam
F	**F**	Claussen

OIL, VINEGAR, OLIVES & PICKLES

WHAT YOU NEED TO KNOW
A number of socially responsible companies now offer conventional and organic oils and vinegars.

BUYING TIPS
✓ Choose organic oil, vinegar & cooking spray

GREEN HERO

Canaan Fair Trade

☆ GAM certified Green Business
☆ The only fair trade certified olives
☆ Supports Palestinian farmers & communities

CORPORATE VILLAIN

Pam (ConAgra)

☠ Massive toxic discharge lawsuit
☠ Food industry "Climate Change Laggard"
☠ #50 in "Top 100 Corporate Criminals"

RESOURCES
🖥 www.canaanfairtrade.com
🖥 www.nutiva.com
🖥 www.edenfoods.com

ONLINE

A	**A+**	
	A	Mozilla, Firefox, Wikipedia, Craigslist, Care2, Red Jellyfish
	A–	Google, Chrome, YouTube
B	**B+**	Apple, Safari
	B	eBay
	B–	AT&T
C	**C+**	Expedia, Orbitz
	C	AOL, Priceline, Facebook, Earthlink, Charter, Qwest, Cablevision
	C–	Blizzard
D	**D+**	Yahoo!, Doubleclick, Flickr
	D	Amazon, MySpace, IMDb
	D–	Comcast, Road Runner
F	**F**	Microsoft, Internet Explorer, MSN, Bing, Live

ONLINE

WHAT YOU NEED TO KNOW

In the information age, what ISP and browser you use is just as important as where you browse. Whenever possible, support those companies and organizations that turn some of your dollars (and clicks) into making a difference on and offline.

BUYING TIPS

✓ Buy local, used items online when possible
✓ Support open source and community efforts

GREEN HERO

Google

☆ 100 Most Ethical Companies list, 3 years
☆ Industry leader in fighting climate change
☆ Perfect 100 on HRC Equality Index, 4 years

CORPORATE VILLAIN

Bing (Microsoft)

☠ CEP "F" for overall social responsibility
☠ Paid $89 million to Washington lobbyists
☠ EC overall responsibility rating of POOR

RESOURCES

💻 www.care2.com
💻 www.redjellyfish.com

PAPER

A	**A+**	New Leaf
	A	Greenline, Living Tree
	A –	
B	**B+**	Mohawk, HP, IBM
	B	Canon, Kodak, Xerox
	B –	3M, Post-It, Staples
C	**C+**	
	C	Great White, Brother, Epson, FedEx Office, Wausau, Smead
	C –	Office Depot
D	**D+**	Hammermill
	D	Avery, Boise Cascade, OfficeMax
	D –	
F	**F**	Mead, Cambridge, Georgia-Pacific

PAPER

WHAT YOU NEED TO KNOW
Just remember one thing: PAPER = TREES.

BUYING TIPS
✓ Look for high post-consumer recycled
   content
✓ Choose non-chlorine bleached paper options
✓ New Leaf paper is now at Kinko's — ask for it

GREEN HERO

New Leaf

☆ Forest Stewardship Council certified
☆ Offers 100% post-consumer options
☆ Invented the Eco-Audit for books, etc.
☆ Uses sustainably harvested wood

CORPORATE VILLAIN

Georgia-Pacific

☠ GP gives lowest environmental ranking
☠ #44 in "Top 100 Corporate Criminals"
☠ Responsible for worst US toxic waste sites
☠ Named global climate change laggard

RESOURCES
🖥 www.newleafpaper.com
🖥 www.greenlinepaper.com

PAPER TOWELS &
TOILET PAPER

A	**A+**	Seventh Generation, Earth Friendly
	A	Green Forest
	A –	
B	**B+**	Natural Value, Marcal, Tork
	B	Scotties, Kleenex, Viva, Scott, Cottonelle, Purely Cotton
	B –	
C	**C+**	Cascades
	C	
	C –	
D	**D+**	International Paper
	D	
	D –	
F	**F**	Georgia Pacific, Quilted Northern, Angel Soft, Dixie, Brawny, Sparkle, Soft n' Gentle, Vanity Fair, Zee, Mardi Gras, Softly, Bounty, Puffs, Charmin, Envision

PAPER TOWELS & TOILET PAPER

WHAT YOU NEED TO KNOW
You can make a lot of difference for our global forests simply by choosing these two items in a responsible manner.

BUYING TIPS
✓ Look for high post-consumer recycled content
✓ Choose non-chlorine bleached paper options
✓ Always buy items with some recycled content

GREEN HERO

Green Forest

☆ GAM certified Green Business
☆ Empowers consumers w/packaging
☆ 100% recycled w/post-consumer content
☆ Humane Certified Producer

CORPORATE VILLAIN

Brawny (Georgia-Pacific)

☠ #44 in "Top 100 Corporate Criminals"
☠ Massive toxic PCB dumping fines
☠ Named global climate change laggard

PASTA & SAUCE

A	**A+**	Eden Foods, Annie's
	A	Amy's
	A–	Muir Glen, DeBoles, Simply Organic, Walnut Acres, Rising Moon, Garden Time, Bionaturae, Seeds of Change
B	**B+**	Lundberg, Newman's Own, Hodgson Mill, Natural Value
	B	Betty Crocker, Golden Grain, Pasta Roni, Progresso
	B–	Prego, Campbell's
C	**C+**	
	C	Barilla, Ronzoni, Stella, McCormick, Emeril's, American Beauty, Emilia, Halbrand, De Cecco, Mezzetta, New World Pasta, Lawry's, Prince, Goya, Manischewitz, DaVinci
	C–	
D	**D+**	Contadina, Classico, Del Monte
	D	Ragu, Bertolli, Knorr
	D–	Chef Boyardee, Hunt's
F	**F**	Kraft, Buitoni, Back To Nature

PASTA & SAUCE

BUYING TIPS
✓ Look for items made with organic ingredients
✓ Buy larger quantities to reduce packaging

GREEN HERO

Lundberg

☆ Use 100% renewable energy in production
☆ Uses organic, sustainable farming practices
☆ No animal testing of its products
☆ Top award for treatment of employees

CORPORATE VILLAIN

Back To Nature (Kraft)

☣ #2 contributor to Washington lobbyists
☣ Greenwash Award for public deception
☣ Undermines overseas health standards
☣ Part of #2 worst company on the earth

RESOURCES
🖥 www.annies.com
🖥 www.muirglen.com
🖥 www.deboles.com
🖥 www.newmansown.com
🖥 www.hodgsonmill.com
🖥 www.lundberg.com

PEANUT BUTTER & JELLY

A	**A+**	Rapunzel
	A	
	A−	Cascadian Farm, Woodstock Farms, Arrowhead Mills, Maranatha, Santa Cruz Organic, Crofter's, Bionaturae, Fiordi Frutta, Kettle Foods
B	**B+**	Smart Balance
	B	Welch's
	B−	
C	**C+**	
	C	Nutella, Joyva, Robertson's, Sorrell Ridge, Bonne Maman, Knott's, Laura Scudder, Smuckers, Adams, Teddie, Jif, Goober, Simply Fruit, Polaner, Manischewitz, Glick's, Lieber's
	C−	
D	**D+**	
	D	Skippy
	D−	Peter Pan
F	**F**	

PEANUT BUTTER & JELLY

BUYING TIPS
✓ Look for items made with organic ingredients
✓ Buy larger quantities to reduce packaging

GREEN HERO
Kettle Foods

☆ 100% of waste oil turned into biodiesel
☆ Restored local wetlands habitat
☆ One of the largest solar arrays in Northwest
☆ Gives tons of potatoes to hunger orgs

CORPORATE VILLAIN
Peter Pan (ConAgra)

☄ Food industry "Climate Change Laggard"
☄ #50 in "Top 100 Corporate Criminals"
☄ 2nd largest E. coli meat recall in history
☄ Many worker safety & health violations

RESOURCES
🖳 www.kettlefoods.com
🖳 www.rapunzel.com
🖳 www.maranathanutbutters.com

PET CARE

A	**A+**	BioBag, Only Natural Pet Store
	A	Natural Life, Swheat Scoop
	A–	Health Valley, Feline Pine, V-Dog, Karma, Pet Promise
B	**B+**	PetGuard, Newman's Own, Halo
	B	Heartland, Zuke's, Sensible Choice, Avoderm, Canidae, Happy Dog, Wellness, Natural Balance
	B–	Castor & Pollux, EVO, Innova
C	**C+**	
	C	PETCO, Jonny Cat, Cat's Pride, Alley Cat, Nylabone
	C–	
D	**D+**	Kibbles 'n Bits, Pounce, Del Monte, 9 Lives, Skippy, Meow Mix, Milk Bone
	D	Hartz, Science Diet, Arm & Hammer
	D–	Greenies, Eukanuba, Cesar, Nutro, Pedigree, Fresh Step, Scoop Away, Royal Canine, Sheba, Whiskas
F	**F**	Purina, Alpo, Fancy Feast, Gourmet, ONE, Friskies, Tender Vittles, IAMS, Chef's Blend, Tidy Cats

PET CARE

WHAT YOU NEED TO KNOW
Recent innovations have been made in the area of socially responsible pet care, so you should have a number of excellent options to choose from.

BUYING TIPS
✓ Buy pet food made with organic ingredients
✓ Buy cat litter made from renewable sources

GREEN HERO

BioBag

☆ 100% biodegradable, corn-based material
☆ 100% compostable w/multiple certifications
☆ GAM certified Green Business

CORPORATE VILLAIN

Purina (Nestle)

☠ "Most Irresponsible" corporation award
☠ Aggressive takeovers of family farms
☠ Involved in child slavery lawsuit

RESOURCES
🖥 www.felinepine.com
🖥 www.onlynaturalpet.com
🖥 www.swheatscoop.com

POPCORN, NUTS, PRETZELS & MIXES

A	**A+**	Equal Exchange
	A	
	A−	SunRidge Farms, Woodstock Farms, Hain, Bearitos, Little Bear
B	**B+**	Newman's Own, Glad Corn, Pirate's Booty, Lesser Evil, Aurora Natural
	B	Snyder's, Pop Secret, True North, Gardetto's, Smartfood, Chex Mix, Cracker Jack, Rold Gold, Emerald, Blue Diamond
	B−	
C	**C+**	
	C	Jolly Time, ExpresSnacks, Yaya's
	C−	
D	**D+**	
	D	
	D−	Act II, Crunch 'n Munch, Jiffy Pop, Orville Redenbacher, Fiddle Faddle, David, Poppycock, Almond Accents
F	**F**	Planters, Corn Nuts

POPCORN, NUTS, PRETZELS & MIXES

WHAT YOU NEED TO KNOW
When you're settling in to watch a little TV or a movie, what you put in that bowl next to the couch makes a big difference for the planet.

BUYING TIPS
✓ Look for items made with organic ingredients

GREEN HERO
Equal Exchange

☆ GAM certified Green Business
☆ Business Ethics Award winner
☆ Industry leader in fair trade movement

CORPORATE VILLAIN
Planters (Kraft)

☣ Part of #2 worst company on the earth
☣ Currently the target of 2 major boycotts
☣ #2 contributor to Washington lobbyists

RESOURCES
💻 www.newmansownorganics.com
💻 www.equalexchange.coop

RETAIL STORES

A	**A+**	Patagonia
	A	
	A–	REI, IKEA
B	**B+**	Timberland
	B	L.L. Bean, Eddie Bauer, Nordstrom, Ace Hardware
	B–	
C	**C+**	
	C	Neiman Marcus, Ross, Best Buy, Dollar General, The North Face, Bed Bath & Beyond
	C–	BJ's
D	**D+**	Target, Lowe's, Talbots, Maytag
	D	Walgreens, CVS, Lowe's, JC Penney
	D–	Marshalls, Macy's, Bloomingdale's, Saks Fifth Avenue, Costco, Kohl's, Rite Aid, Home Depot, Osco, Sav-On, Supervalu
F	**F**	Wal-Mart, Sam's Club, Sears, Kmart, Big Lots, Orchard Supply Hardware, Land's End, Dillard's

RETAIL STORES

GREEN HERO

Patagonia

☆ Environmental leader in industry
☆ Plastic bottles recycling pioneer — fleece
☆ 1% of sales goes to enviro groups
☆ Powered by 100% renewable energy

GREEN HERO

IKEA

☆ Works with UNICEF & Greenpeace
☆ Uses no timber from natural forests
☆ Involved in affordable housing efforts
☆ Funds efforts to stop international child labor

CORPORATE VILLAIN

Walmart

☠ #3 worst company on the planet
☠ CEP "F" for overall social responsibility
☠ Sex-discrimination class-action lawsuit
☠ Documented exploitation of child labor
☠ Paid $27 million to Washington lobbyists

RESOURCES
🖥 www.patagonia.com
🖥 www.rei.com

RICE & OTHER GRAINS

	A+	Eden Foods, AlterEco
A	A	Fantastic Foods
	A–	Near East, Seeds Of Change, Casbah
	B+	Lundberg, Annie Chun's
B	B	Betty Crocker, Rice-A-Roni, Quaker, Bac-Os
	B–	
	C+	
C	C	Carolina, Goya, Success Rice, Lipton, Mahatma, Minute Rice, Dynasty, S&W, Manischewitz, Hungry Jack, Mrs. Cubbison's, McCormick
	C–	
	D+	Hormel
D	D	Knorr
	D–	Uncle Ben's
F	F	Kraft

RICE & OTHER GRAINS

BUYING TIPS
✓ Look for organic grains
✓ Buy in bulk to reduce packaging waste

GREEN HERO

AlterEco

☆ Produces a range of 100% fair trade goods
☆ Works directly with local farmer cooperatives
☆ GAM certified Green Business
☆ Fair trade consumer education leader

CORPORATE VILLAIN

Uncle Ben's (Mars)

☠ On MM's "10 Worst Corporations" list
☠ Evidence that suppliers use child slave labor
☠ Target of fair trade campaign
☠ CEP "F" for overall social responsibility

RESOURCES
🖥 www.altereco-usa.com
🖥 www.edenfoods.com
🖥 www.fantasticfoods.com
🖥 www.seedsofchange.com

SALAD DRESSINGS & TOPPINGS

A	**A+**	
	A	Annie's Naturals
	A−	Spectrum, Edward & Sons, Seeds of Change, OrganicVille, Follow Your Heart
B	**B+**	Nasoya, Newman's Own, Bragg
	B	
	B−	Pepperidge Farm
C	**C+**	
	C	Bernstein's, Brianna's, Drew's, Mrs. Cubbison's, Cardini's, Ken's Steak House, Girard's, Fresh Gourmet, Calbec, Marzetti, Marie's, Mezzetta, Maple Grove Farms, Hidden Valley
	C−	
D	**D+**	
	D	Wish-Bone
	D−	Marie Callender's, French's
F	**F**	Kraft, Good Seasons

SALAD DRESSINGS & TOPPINGS

WHAT YOU NEED TO KNOW
While there are still only a handful of socially responsible companies in this category, they offer a wide variety of salad dressings.

BUYING TIPS
✓ Buy dressing made with organic ingredients

GREEN HERO
Annie's Naturals
☆ Supports organic, family farms
☆ Created environmental studies scholarship
☆ GAM certified Green Business
☆ Regularly donates products to nonprofits

CORPORATE VILLAIN
Good Seasons (Kraft)
☠ Part of #2 worst company on the earth
☠ Named global climate change laggard
☠ Undermines overseas health standards

RESOURCES
🖥 www.anniesnaturals.com
🖥 www.followyourheart.com

SALSA, SPREADS & DIPS

A	**A+**	
	A	Emerald Valley, Wildwood, Amy's
	A−	Walnut Acres, Bearitos, Rising Moon, Seeds Of Change, Muir Glen
B	**B+**	Newman's Own, 505, Casa Sanchez
	B	Tostitos, Lay's, Fritos, Old El Paso
	B−	Sabra
C	**C+**	Pace
	C	Nonna Lena's, Salpica, Frontera, Chi Chi's, Raquel's, Gringo, Native, Mrs. Renfro's, Micaelas, Green Mountain, Ortega, Litehouse, Margaritaville, La Victoria, Haig's, Cedar's, Laura Scudder's
	C−	
D	**D+**	
	D	
	D−	Rosarita
F	**F**	Taco Bell, Kraft

SALSA, SPREADS & DIPS

WHAT YOU NEED TO KNOW
This category includes everything from hummus to salsa to bean dip, and there are responsible choices to be had for every one.

GREEN HERO

Emerald Valley

☆ Socially Responsible Business Award
☆ 1% to humanitarian & ecological causes
☆ Green Business Of The Year Award

CORPORATE VILLAIN

Taco Bell (Kraft)

☠ Named "Top 10 Greenwasher"
☠ Involved in document deletion cover-up
☠ Continues to do business in Burma
☠ Spent over $178* million on lobbyists

RESOURCES
🖥 www.emeraldvalleykitchen.com
🖥 www.amyskitchen.com
🖥 www.seedsofchange.com

SEAFOOD I

A	**A+**	Henry & Lisa's, EcoFish
	A	Wildcatch, Wild Planet, VitalChoice, Pelican's Choice
	A-	Natural Sea, Blue Horizon Organic, RainCoast
B	**B+**	Trader Joe's*
	B	Contessa, Bela, Omega
	B-	Ahold*, Wegmans*
C	**C+**	Whole Foods*, Target*
	C	Flott, Deep Sea, Chicken of the Sea, Bumble Bee, King Oscar, Beach Cliff, Van de Kamp's, Geisha, Ola!, Crown Prince, Snow's, Brunswick, Vince's, Star, Gorton's, Lascco, Flott, Jensen's, Swanson, Louis Kemp
	C-	Walmart*
D	**D+**	Starkist, Delhaize*
	D	Kroger*, Costco*, Aldi*
	D-	A&P*, Supervalu*
F	**F**	Giant Eagle*, Publix*, Winn-Dixie*, Meijer*, Price Chopper*, H.E. Butt*

SEAFOOD I

WHAT YOU NEED TO KNOW

One of the most important changes you can make is in choosing ecologically responsible seafood. Supermarkets are rated here solely based on their seafood sustainability and are noted with an asterisk.

BUYING TIPS

✓ Look for labels evidencing sustainable fishing
✓ Local freshwater is often a good choice
✓ See next section for more seafood guidance

GREEN HERO

Henry & Lisa's

☆ Only environmentally sustainable fishing
☆ Conservation scientists advisory board
☆ Result of marine conservation groups

GREEN HERO

Wildcatch

☆ Certified by Marine Stewardship Council
☆ Harvests only sustainable, wild seafood
☆ Works with nonprofits like Salmon Nation

RESOURCES

🖳 www.ecofish.com
🖳 www.wildcatch.com

SEAFOOD II

A	A	Wild Alaskan Salmon, Arctic Char, Mackerel, Striped Bass, Sardines, Anchovies, Abalone, Mussels, Giant Clam, Dungeness & Stone Crab
B	B	Pacific Halibut, Black Cod, Catfish, Clams, Oysters, Prawns, Scallops, Squid, Tilapia, Trout, Sablefish
C	C	Tuna (except Bluefin), Pacific Cod, King Crab, Blue Crab, Lobster, Sea Urchin, Shrimp, Crayfish, Herring, Washington Salmon, Mahi-Mahi, Pollock
D	D	Flounder, Haddock, Rockfish, Caviar, Sole, Swordfish
F	F	Chilean Sea Bass, Monkfish, Orange Roughy, Snapper, Atlantic Cod, Atlantic Halibut, Farmed & Atlantic Salmon, Bluefin Tuna, Octopus, Shark, Skate, Eel, Marlin, Grouper

SEAFOOD II

WHAT YOU NEED TO KNOW
Our current fishing practices are destroying
ocean life at an unprecedented rate. Rather
than ranking companies, the chart to the left
shows which species are being more sustainably harvested and which are being fished out
of existence based on a synthesis of available
data from the major organizations researching
this issue. It also takes into account the
environmental costs of harvesting each kind
of seafood. Use it at both the supermarket
seafood counter and when you go out to eat.

BUYING TIPS
✓ When it's unclear, ask the deli staffer or server
   for more specifics about the fish
✓ When A or B category seafood is not available, consider non-seafood alternatives

RESOURCES
🖥 www.seafoodwatch.org
🖥 www.oceansalive.org/eat.cfm
🖥 www.blueocean.org/seafood
🖥 www.msc.org

SHOES

A	A+	Dansko, Ecolution, Blackspot, Autonomie Project, Patagonia
	A	UGG, Teva, Simple Shoes
	A−	Earth Shoes, Birkenstock
B	B+	Timberland
	B	Chaco, Red Wing
	B−	Reebok, DMX, Rockport
C	C+	Nike, Adidas, DC
	C	Ecco, North Face, Salomon, HI-TEC, Crocs, Keen, Merrell, Umbro, FILA, Ellesse, Zappos
	C−	Brooks, Lotto
D	D+	K-Swiss, Puma, New Balance
	D	Foot Locker, Pentland, Keds, Sperry, Tommy Hilfiger
	D−	Vans, ASICS, Converse, Nunn Bush, Florsheim, Mizuno, Stride Rite, Saucony, Skechers
F	F	LA Gear, Reef, DISCOUNT & DEPARTMENT STORE BRANDS

SHOES

WHAT YOU NEED TO KNOW

Almost all store-bought shoes are made in factories in the developing world. The real question is: how are the workers treated, are they safe, and do they make enough of a wage to live decently? Your choices here will determine the answers to those questions for thousands.

GREEN HERO

Dansko

☆ GAM certified Green Business
☆ Powered by 100% renewable energy
☆ LEED Gold eco-certified main office

CORPORATE VILLAIN

LA Gear

☠ Named "Sweatshop Laggard"
☠ CEP "F" for overall social responsibility
☠ No supplier code of conduct for workers

RESOURCES

🖥 www.simpleshoes.com
🖥 www.ecolution.com
🖥 www.blackspotsneaker.org
🖥 www.dansko.com
🖥 www.autonomieproject.com

SOAP

A	**A+**	Dr. Bronner's, Method
	A	Tom's of Maine, Juniper Ridge
	A–	Aubrey Organics, Kiss My Face, EO, Simmons, Organic Options
B	**B+**	Jäsön, Sappo Hill, River Soap, Alba, Zum Bar, Nature's Gate, Plantlife, Shikai, Earth Therapeutics, Moon Valley, One With Nature, HUGO
	B	Avalon, Irish Spring, Softsoap
	B–	Aveeno, Purell
C	**C+**	St. Ive's, Clearly Natural
	C	Burt's Bees, Germ-X
	C–	Coastal
D	**D+**	Nivea
	D	Dove, Suave, Axe, Lever, Caress
	D–	
F	**F**	Dial, Coast, Tone, Pure & Natural, Ivory, Safeguard, Olay, Zest, Old Spice, Lava, Gillette

SOAP

BUYING TIPS
✓ Choose soaps that aren't tested on animals
✓ Buy soaps with less or recyclable packaging

GREEN HERO

Dr. Bronner's

☆ Leader in organic standards integrity
☆ 5:1 CEO to worker salary cap
☆ Profits donated to variety of causes
☆ Liquid soaps in 100% recycled plastic
☆ Does not test on animals

CORPORATE VILLAIN

Dial

☠ Continues unnecessary animal testing
☠ CEP "F" for overall social responsibility
☠ Refuses disclosure to consumers
☠ Sexual discrimination/harassment suits

RESOURCES
🖳 www.drbronner.com
🖳 www.tomsofmaine.com
🖳 www.aubreyorganics.com
🖳 www.juniperridge.com

SODA

A	**A+**	
	A	Steaz, Maine Root, Java Pop
	A −	Santa Cruz Organic, Chill
B	**B+**	Reed's, Virgil's, Blue Sky, Hansen's, Newman's Own, Jones, RW Knudsen
	B	Bundaberg, Thomas Kemper, Izze, Crystal Geyser, The Switch, Sierra Mist, Tropicana, Mug, Pepsi, Slice, Mountain Dew
	B −	Orangina, 7-Up, Snapple, A&W, Diet Rite, Squirt, Sunkist, Welch's, IBC, Stewart's, Dr Pepper, Schweppes, Canada Dry, Crush, RC Cola
C	**C +**	Henry Weinhard's
	C	Shasta, Jolt, Faygo, Boylan, Bawls, Polar, Moxie, Arizona
	C −	Weight Watchers
D	**D+**	
	D	Lipton
	D −	
F	**F**	Coca-Cola, Sprite, Fanta, Pibb Xtra, Barq's, Minute Maid, San Pellegrino, Fresca, Tab

SODA

WHAT YOU NEED TO KNOW
If you're like most people, soda is a daily part of your diet. Move up on the responsible soda chain to avoid companies that are wrecking the planet.

BUYING TIPS
✓ Buy soda in aluminum or glass containers

GREEN HERO

Steaz

☆ Organic drinks industry leader
☆ Profits donated to Sri Lankan village
☆ Supports sustainable farming practices
☆ Offers fair trade certified sodas

CORPORATE VILLAIN

Coca-Cola

☠ MM's "Worst Corporation" list for 3 years
☠ Hinders clean water access abroad
☠ Target of major human rights boycotts

RESOURCES
🖥 www.steaz.com
🖥 www.javapop.com/javapop.swf
🖥 www.reedsgingerbrew.com

SOUPS, NOODLES & CURRIES

A	**A+**	Eden Foods, Rapunzel, Annie's
	A	Amy's, Fantastic Foods
	A–	Walnut Acres, Imagine, Casbah, Nile Spice, Health Valley, Edward & Sons, Organic Planet, Native Forest, Ginger People, Seeds of Change, Shelton's, Muir Glen
B	**B+**	Annie Chun's, Pacific Natural, Dr. McDougall's, Nasoya, Spice Hunter
	B	Progresso
	B–	Campbell's, Wolfgang Puck
C	**C+**	
	C	Bear Creek, Maruchan, Nissin, Thai Kitchen, Swanson, Tasty Bite, Sun Luck Alessi, Snow's, Bar Harbor
	C–	
D	**D+**	Mrs. Grass, Herb Ox
	D	Knorr, Lipton
	D–	Healthy Choice
F	**F**	

SOUPS, NOODLES & CURRIES

WHAT YOU NEED TO KNOW
Whether it's instant noodles or pea soup, there are many excellent choices for hot, steaming, socially responsible meals.

BUYING TIPS
✓ Look for soups made with organic ingredients

GREEN HERO

Rapunzel

☆ Fair trade & organic leader in food ind.
☆ Supports global sustainable farming
☆ Produced 1st 100% organic chocolate

CORPORATE VILLAIN

Healthy Choice (ConAgra)

☠ Food industry "Climate Change Laggard"
☠ MM's "Worst Corporation" list for 2 years
☠ #50 in "Top 100 Corporate Criminals"

RESOURCES
🖳 www.rapunzel.com
🖳 www.fantasticfoods.com
🖳 www.amyskitchen.com

SUGAR, SPICES & SWEETENERS

A	**A+**	Wholesome Sweeteners, Eden Foods, AlterEco, King Arthur, Equal Exchange
	A	Frontier, Simply Organic, Silk Road, Great Northern, Coombs
	A–	NOW, Hain, Florida Crystals, Spicely
B	**B+**	Spice Hunter, Lundberg, Bragg
	B	Spice Islands
	B–	Splenda
C	**C+**	Molly McButter, Sugar Twin, Dash
	C	C&H, Domino, Sweet 'N Low, Butter Buds, McCormick, Sugar in the Raw, Spike, Morton, Mrs. Butterworth's, Goya
	C–	
D	**D+**	Hormel
	D	Lawry's, Adolph's
	D–	Equal, Nutrasweet
F	**F**	

SUGAR, SPICES & SWEETENERS

WHAT YOU NEED TO KNOW
Many of these items we buy once and keep using for years. If you want to make a difference while saving your budget, start here.

BUYING TIPS
✓ Buy in bulk to reduce packaging waste

GREEN HERO

Wholesome Sweeteners

☆ 1st US fair trade certified sugar available
☆ Actively supports sustainable farming
☆ Makes a full line of organic sweeteners

CORPORATE VILLAIN

Hormel

☠ Supports inhumane factory farming
☠ Low score on HRC Equality Index
☠ Refuses disclosure to consumers

RESOURCES
🖥 www.wholesomesweeteners.com
🖥 www.frontiercoop.com
🖥 www.altereco-usa.com

SUPERMARKETS

A	A+	FOOD CO-OPS, FARMERS MARKETS
	A	
	A–	Whole Foods, Wild Oats
B	B+	Trader Joe's
	B	Wegmans, Nugget
	B–	Raley's, Fresh & Easy, Harris Teeter, Stop & Shop, Giant
C	C+	Peapod, Pathmark
	C	Shop 'n Save, Food Lion, A&P, Weis
	C–	Von's, Fry's, Pak 'n' Save, ShopRite, Safeway, Roundys, BJ's, Tom Thumb
D	D+	Hannaford, Giant Eagle, Target
	D	Price Chopper, Price Mart, H.E.B., Walgreen, CVS, Long's, Thriftway
	D–	Meijer, Winn-Dixie, Albertsons, Cub, Acme, Bigg's, Jewel-Osco, Lucky's, Save-A-Lot, Shaw's, Star, Publix, Costco, Shoppers, SuperValu, Super Saver, Rite Aid
F	F	Walmart, Ralph's, Food 4 Less, QFC, Fred Meyer, King Soopers, Kwik Shop, Quick Stop, Kroger, Smith's

SUPERMARKETS

WHAT YOU NEED TO KNOW

If you have a choice, changing where you shop is an incredibly powerful action that will support people and the planet above profit.

GREEN HERO

Whole Foods

☆ BE's "Best Corporations" list for 3 years
☆ Powered by 100% renewable energy
☆ Business Ethics Award winner
☆ Established animal & poverty foundation
☆ Created animal compassion standards

CORPORATE VILLAIN

Wal-Mart

☠ MM's "Worst Corporation" list for 3 years
☠ Major toxic waste dumping fines
☠ CEP "F" for overall social responsibility
☠ Documented exploitation of child labor
☠ #3 worst company on the planet

RESOURCES

Find food co-ops & farmers' markets
⌨ www.localharvest.org
⌨ www.cooperativegrocer.coop

TEA

A	**A+**	Traditional Medicinals, Numi, Equal Exchange, Choice, Honest Tea, Guayaki
	A	Zhena's Gypsy, Leaf Spa, Eco Teas, Arbor, Tulsi, Organic India, Rishi, Art of Tea, Davidson's, Oregon Chai
	A−	Yogi, Third Street Chai, Tao Of Tea, Celestial Seasonings
B	**B+**	Republic Of Tea, Sweet Leaf, Mighty Leaf, Pacific Natural, Bionaturae, Jones, Newman's Own
	B	Tazo, Pixie Mate, Tejava, Stash
	B−	Snapple
C	**C+**	Bigelow
	C	Harney & Sons, Triple Leaf, Itoen, Coffee Bean & Tea Leaf, Arizona
	C−	Red Rose
D	**D+**	Tetley, Good Earth, Twinings
	D	Lipton
	D−	
F	**F**	Nestea

TEA

WHAT YOU NEED TO KNOW
If you drink tea, you have an incredible selection of human and planet friendly varieties to pick from.

BUYING TIPS
✓ Look first and foremost for the fair trade label

GREEN HERO
Numi

☆ GAM certified Green Business
☆ Member of the Social Venture Network
☆ Socially Responsible Business Award

GREEN HERO
Honest Tea

☆ GAM certified Green Business
☆ Ranked #16 best company on the planet
☆ Awarded "Most Democratic Workplace"

RESOURCES
🖳 www.equalexchange.com
🖳 www.taooftea.com
🖳 www.honesttea.com

TOYS & GAMES

A	**A+**	
	A	Hazelnut Kids, Down to Earth Toys, Eco Toy Town
	A –	Wild Planet, Tree Hollow
B	**B+**	Sony, Playstation, Hot Wheels, Mattel
	B	
	B –	
C	**C+**	Electronic Arts, Toys R Us, Crayola
	C	Fisher Price, Wham-O, Lego, GameStop
	C –	Blizzard, Activision
D	**D+**	
	D	
	D –	Nintendo, Wii
F	**F**	Microsoft, Xbox, Playskool, Hasbro, Parker Brothers, Play-Doh, Disney, Tonka, Nerf

TOYS & GAMES

WHAT YOU NEED TO KNOW
The irresponsible manufacturing of toys and games does not always directly threaten us or our children, but it always endangers people or the environment in some part of the world.

BUYING TIPS
✓ Look for less common, cooperative games
✓ Buy used toys & games when available
✓ Seek out shareware & open source games

CORPORATE VILLAIN

Hasbro

☠ Low score on HRC Equality Index
☠ Named "Sweatshop Laggard" by CEP
☠ No code of conduct for factories abroad

CORPORATE VILLAIN

Xbox (Microsoft)

☠ CEP "F" for overall social responsibility
☠ Named "abusive monopoly" by US Court
☠ Greenpeace "Green Electronics Laggard"
☠ Paid $89 million to Washington lobbyists

RESOURCES
🖳 www.wildplanet.com
🖳 www.seriousgames.org

VITAMINS

A	**A+**	
	A	New Chapter Organics
	A−	NOW Foods, Oregon's Wild Harvest, Spectrum
B	**B+**	Rainbow Light
	B	Nature's Way
	B−	Viactiv
C	**C+**	Sundown Naturals
	C	Nature's Life, Solaray, VegiLife, GNC, Natrol, SuperNutrition, Solgar, All One, Nature Made, Emergen-C, Weil, Twinlab, Nature's Plus, Nature's Bounty, Source Naturals, Country Life, Wellesse, Carlson, Jarrow
	C−	
D	**D+**	
	D	
	D−	One-A-Day, Flinstones, Bayer
F	**F**	Centrum

VITAMINS

BUYING TIPS
✓ Look for organic ingredients in supplements
✓ Buy in recyclable bottles: #1, #2, or glass
✓ Purchase in bulk to reduce packaging waste

GREEN HERO
New Chapter Organics

☆ Organic, sustainable, harvesting practices
☆ International biodynamic certification
☆ Extensive environmental awards
☆ Promotes efforts to sustain biodiversity

GREEN HERO
NOW

☆ Reduced waste by 50% in 3 years
☆ Donates to WWF & Second Harvest
☆ Environmental & Sustainability Awards
☆ Industry leader in recycling efforts

CORPORATE VILLAIN
Centrum (Wyeth)

☠ MM's "Worst Corporation" list for 2 years
☠ Target of major animal welfare boycott
☠ Numerous federal ethics violations
☠ Responsible for EPA Superfund site
☠ #93 in "Top 100 Corporate Criminals"

WATER

A	**A+**	TAP / FILTERED
	A	
	A−	Earth Water, Biota
B	**B+**	Ethos, Voss, Balance
	B	Crystal Geyser, Metro Mint, Propel, Aquafina, SoBe
	B−	Deja Blue, Dannon, Evian, Volvic, Schweppes, Snapple
C	**C+**	K2O
	C	La Croix, Hawaii, Ice Age, Icelandic Glacial, Fiji, Penta, Trinity, Fruit2O, Saratoga, Essentia, Crystal Springs, Sparkletts, Adirondack, Arizona
	C−	
D	**D+**	
	D	
	D−	
F	**F**	Glaceau, Vitamin Water, Arrowhead, Smart Water, Dasani, Vittel, Perrier, Deer Park, Calistoga, S. Pellegrino, Vittel, Poland Spring, Zephyr Hills, Ozarka, Ice Mountain, Acqua Panna

WATER

BUYING TIPS
✓ Carry your own reusable bottle
✓ Buy fewer, larger bottles, and refill them
✓ ALWAYS recycle the bottles when done

GREEN HERO

Earth Water

☆ 100% of profits donated to UNHCR
☆ Biodegradable water bottle

CORPORATE VILLAIN

Arrowhead (Nestle)

☠ "Most Irresponsible" corporation award
☠ Baby formula human rights boycott
☠ Involved in child slavery lawsuit

CORPORATE VILLAIN

Dasani (Coca Cola)

☠ Hinders clean water access abroad
☠ MM's "Worst Corporation" list for 3 years
☠ Target of major human rights boycotts

RESOURCES
🖥 www.earthwater.ca
🖥 www.ethoswater.com

WINE

A	A+	LOCAL VINEYARDS
	A	Frey, Fetzer, La Rocca, Frog's Leap
	A−	Lolonis, Honeyrun, Kunde Estate, Alma Rosa, French Rabbit
B	B+	Banrock Station, Rodney Strong, Sobon Estate, St. Francis
	B	Mountain Meadows, Bota Box, Cline
	B−	Sutter Home
C	C+	Franzia, Ecco Domani, Luna di Luna, Turning Leaf, Gallo, Carlo Rossi, Beringer
	C	Lindemans, Almaden, KWV, Kendall Jackson, Jacob's Creek, Woodbridge, Lindemans, Bogle, Balbo, Inglenook, Glen Ellen, Columbia Crest, Delicato
	C−	Charles Shaw, Barefoot, Yellow Tail, Corbett Canyon, Duckhorn, Mondavi
D	D+	Sterling, Blossom Hill
	D	Dom Perignon, Krug, Cloudy Bay
	D−	
F	F	Stag's Leap, Chateau Ste Michelle

WINE

BUYING TIPS
✓ Look for organic wine varieties on the shelf
✓ Support local vineyards — try their wine
✓ Buy in bulk to reduce packaging waste

GREEN HERO
Fetzer

☆ Powered by 100% renewable energy
☆ All vineyards certified organic
☆ Reduced production waste by 94%
☆ Bottles are 40% recycled glass
☆ BE Award for Environmental Excellence

GREEN HERO
Frey

☆ GAM certified Green Business
☆ Oldest organic US winery
☆ 1st US biodynamic wine producer

RESOURCES
🖳 www.fetzer.com
🖳 www.freywine.com
🖳 www.frogsleap.com

PRODUCT CATEGORY INDEX

Lip Balm	Body Care
Margarine	Butter & Margarine
Marshmallows	Baked Goods & Baking Supplies
Mayonnaise	Condiments
Mobile Phones	Cell Phones & Service
Mouthwash	Dental Care
Mustard	Condiments
Noodles	Soup, Noodles & Curries
Nuts	Popcorn, Nuts, Pretzels & Mixes
Package Delivery	Office Supplies
Pain Relievers	Medical
Pancake Mix	Breakfast Food
Pencils & Pens	Office Supplies
Pickles	Oil, Vinegar, Olives & Pickles
Pies	Desserts
Pizza	Frozen Dinners
Potato Chips	Chips
Pretzels	Popcorn, Nuts, Pretzels & Mixes
Pudding	Dairy Products
Relishes	Oil, Vinegar, Olives & Pickles
Rice Milk	Milk & Alternatives
Salt	Sugar, Spices & Sweeteners
School Supplies	Office Supplies
Shampoo	Hair Care

Shaving Needs	Body Care
Shortening	Oil, Vinegar, Olives & Pickles
Soft Drinks	Soda
Soy Milk	Milk & Alternatives
Sports Drinks	Energy Drinks
Stuffing Mix	Bread
Sun Block	Body Care
Syrup	Sugar, Spices & Sweeteners
Tahini	Peanut Butter & Jelly
Tampons	Feminine Care
Tape	Office Supplies
Tissues	Paper Towels & Toilet Paper
Tofu	Meat Alternatives
Toilet Paper	Paper Towels & Toilet Paper
Tomato Paste	Pasta & Sauce
Toothbrushes	Dental Care
Toothpaste	Dental Care
Tuna	Seafood
Veggie Burgers	Meat Alternatives
Vinegar	Oil, Vinegar, Olives & Pickles
Video Games	Toys & Games
Waffles	Breakfast Food
Whipped Cream	Dairy Products
Yogurt	Dairy Products

DATA SOURCES

1. American Humane [americanhumane.org]
2. B Corporation [bcorporation.net]
3. Berne Declaration [evb.ch/en]
4. Better World Shopper [betterworldshopper.org]
5. Business Ethics [business-ethics.com]
6. Business for Social Responsibility [bsr.org]
7. Caring Consumer [caringconsumer.com]
8. Center for Public Integrity [publicintegrity.org]
9. Center For Responsive Politics [opensecrets.org]
10. CERES Principles [ceres.org]
11. Clean Clothes Campaign [cleanclothes.org]
12. Clean Computer Campaign [svtc.igc.org/cleancc]
13. Clean Up Fashion [cleanupfashion.co.uk]
14. Climate Counts [climatecounts.org]
15. Cornucopia Institute [cornucopia.org]
16. Corporate Accountability International
      [stopcorporateabuse.org]
17. Corporate Knights [corporateknights.ca]
18. Corpwatch [corpwatch.org]
19. Covalence EthicalQuote [covalence.ch]
20. CSRwire [csrwire.com]
21. Electronics TakeBack Coalition
      [electronicstakeback.com]
22. Ethical Consumer [ethicalconsumer.org]
23. Ethisphere [ethisphere.com]
24. Fair Trade Federation [fairtradefederation.org]
25. Fast Company [fastcompany.com]
26. Forest Ethics [forestethics.org]

DATA SOURCES

27. FTSE4Good Global Index [ftse4good.com]
28. Global Sullivan Principles
    [thesullivanfoundation.org/gsp]
29. Green America [greenamerica.org]
30. Green Cross International [gci.ch]
31. Green-e [green-e.org]
32. Greenopia [greenopia.com]
33. Greenpeace [greenpeace.org]
34. Hoover's [hoovers.com]
35. Human Rights Campaign [hrc.org]
36. Know More [knowmore.org]
37. Maquila Solidarity Network [maquilasolidarity.org]
38. Multinational Monitor [multinationalmonitor.org]
39. Natural Resources Defense Council [nrdc.org]
40. Organic Consumers Assn [organicconsumers.org]
41. New York Times [newyorktimes.com]
42. Political Economy Research Institute
       [peri.umass.edu]
43. Responsible Shopper [responsibleshopper.org]
44. Social Venture Network [svn.org]
45. Socially Responsible Business Awards
       [sociallyresponsiblebusinessawards.org]
46. Transfair USA [transfairusa.org]
47. Union of Concerned Scientists [ucsusa.org]
48. U.S. Environmental Protection Agency [epa.gov]
49. Washington Post [washingtonpost.com]
50. WorldBlu [worldblu.com]
51. World Environment Center [wec.org]
52. World Wildlife Fund [worldwildlife.org]

About the Author

Since receiving his doctoral degree in sociology from the University of Colorado, Boulder, Ellis Jones has focused all of his energies on bridging the gap between academics, activists and the average citizen. A scholar of social responsibility, global citizenship and everyday activism, Dr. Jones continues to teach and give presentations across the country on how to turn lofty ideals into practical actions. His other works include *The Better World Handbook* (winner of *Spirituality & Health*'s Best Book of the Year Award for 2002 under the category of Hope) and his forth-coming book, *The Social Responsibility Movement: Global Transformation In Every-day Life.*

Dr. Jones has given inspiring yet practi-cal presentations to a wide variety of audi-ences including a number of colleges and universities, sustainability symposiums, and global citizenship summits. He has been interviewed for radio and television in both the US and Canada, and was fea-tured in the documentary film, *50 Ways To Save The Planet.* In 2005, his work inspired the creation of The Better World Handbook Festival in Vancouver, BC. He has lived, studied and worked in many parts of Europe, Asia and Central America.

He has won numerous awards for his work in the classroom and currently teaches in the Social Transformation pro-gram at Saybrook Graduate School and the Department of Sociology & Anthropology at Holy Cross College in Worcester, MA.

If you are interested in learning more about his work or would like to schedule a speaking engagement, please send an email to:

doctorjones@betterworldshopper.org

If you have enjoyed *The Better World Shopping Guide*
you might also enjoy other

BOOKS TO BUILD A NEW SOCIETY

Our books provide positive solutions for people who want to
make a difference. We specialize in:

**Environment and Justice • Conscientious Commerce
Sustainable Living • Ecological Design and Planning
Natural Building & Appropriate Technology • Nonviolence
Educational and Parenting Resources • Progressive Leadership**

New Society Publishers
ENVIRONMENTAL BENEFITS STATEMENT

New Society Publishers has chosen to produce this book on Enviro
100, recycled paper made with **100% post consumer waste**,
processed chlorine free, and old growth free.

For every 5,000 books printed, New Society saves the following
resources:[1]

9	Trees
788	Pounds of Solid Waste
867	Gallons of Water
1,130	Kilowatt Hours of Electricity
1,432	Pounds of Greenhouse Gases
6	Pounds of HAPs, VOCs, and AOX Combined
2	Cubic Yards of Landfill Space

[1]Environmental benefits are calculated based on research done by the
Environmental Defense Fund and other members of the Paper Task Force
who study the environmental impacts of the paper industry.

For a full list of NSP's titles, please call **1-800-567-6772**
or check out our website at: **www.newsociety.com**

NEW SOCIETY PUBLISHERS

BOOKS TO BUILD A NEW SOCIETY

New Society Publishers

P.O. Box 189

Gabriola Island,

B.C. V0R 1X0

Canada

Our books provide positive solutions for people who want to make a difference.

For a copy of our catalog, please mail this card to us. We specialize in:

+ Activism
+ Globalization
+ Ecological Design & Planning
+ Environment & Economy

+ Conscientious Commerce
+ Sustainable Living
+ Environmental Education
+ Education & Parenting

+ Progressive Leadership
+ Conflict Education
+ Natural Building & Renewable Energy

☐ *Please subscribe me to* New Society News — *our monthly e-mail newsletter.*

Name _____

Address/City/Province _____

Postal Code/Zip _____ Email Address _____

toll-free 800-567-6772

New Society Publishers

www.newsociety.com